WP

6/06

'It brings into v...   ... Tibetan people –
Soname Yangche ...   ... this touching and
beautiful book is ...underpinned by the steely bravery and humour
of her race.'

Joanna Lumley

Child of *Tibet*

THE STORY OF SONAME'S
FLIGHT TO FREEDOM

SONAME YANGCHEN
with VICKI MACKENZIE

PORTRAIT

Copyright © 2006 by Soname Yangchen and Vicki Mackenzie

First published in Great Britain in 2006 by
Piatkus Books Ltd
5 Windmill Street
London W1T 2JA
e-mail: info@piatkus.co.uk

The moral rights of the authors have been asserted

A catalogue record for this book is available from the British Library

ISBN 0 7499 5111 7

This book has been printed on paper manufactured
with respect for the environment using wood from
managed sustainable resources

Data manipulation by
Action Publishing Technology Ltd, Gloucester
Printed & bound in Great Britain by
MPG Books, Bodmin, Cornwall

To Deckyi

And to the Dalai Lama and the Tibetan people

A Message From My Heart

As you will see as you read my book, life can be quite tough in Dharamsala, especially when one has little resources. That rings especially true when it comes to healthcare. The closest Western standard hospitals are in Chandigarh or New Delhi, respectively six or ten hours journey away, a trip and treatment only the wealthy can afford. For the poor, who make up the majority, the situation can be grave.

That's why I decided to initiate the Gyuto Tantric University Hospital project, to provide first class medical care for the local population of Himachal Pradesh, be they Indian or Tibetan, Muslim, Hindu, Sikh, Buddhist etc., regardless of caste or creed.

When my friends Dr. Claus and Dr. Hedda Blumenroth retired from their work, they donated all the equipment from their private hospital to this noble cause.

We have just returned from Dharamsala where the nine trucks carrying more than 5000 items have safely arrived.

We now urgently need to raise about $750,000 to acquire land adjacent to the Gyuto Monastery and to complete the 50 bed facility, housing two operating theatres, and also to fund two resident practitioners of traditional Tibetan medicine.

Our project carries the blessings of both Their Holinesses The Dalai Lama and Gyalwa Karmapa.

Any generous donations are deeply appreciated and are a great way to accumulate countless merit by fulfilling Their Holinesses' vision of this selfless altruistic project.

Please visit www.soname.com/charities.html, www.roterlotus. org, and www.gtuh.org, for more information on how you can help.

Many Thanks from Soname

Contents

Acknowledgements

First of all I would like to thank His Holiness the Dalai Lama, for without Him this book would never have been written, as it was He who thrust Tibet on to the world stage and got people interested in our culture.

I would also like to thank Vicki Mackenzie, who is a tremendous listener. We cried a lot together while working on the story.

Also of great help were Mr Tashi Tsering of Amnye Machen Institute, a sublime scholar and walking encyclopedia of Tibetan History, and his translator friend Mr Sonam Tsering of the Library of Tibetan Works and Archives. Thank you also to Byron Allen for sending me his poem, which is reproduced in Chapter 13.

Big thanks also to my agent Ivan Mulcahy and everybody at Piatkus for believing in me.

CHAPTER ONE

Wild Beginnings

I WAS BORN WHILE MY mother was milking in a windy cow-shed, in the wild countryside of Yarlung, south central Tibet. An hour later the cow herself gave birth. This was seen as an auspicious sign, and I was given the name Soname, meaning 'Good Fortune', because I had the choice of my mother's milk and the cow's, and Yangchen, meaning 'Melody', because it was festival season when everyone sang. The name was run together and I was called Soname Yangchen all through my early years. My birth was probably in spring 1973, though nobody knows for sure. The West is fixated on age, but we Tibetans don't care about birthdays. When I was born, birth certificates did not even exist. We all simply became another year older every New Year.

In spite of my fortunate name I could not have been born at a more calamitous time or place. Tibet in 1973 was right in the middle of the Cultural Revolution, when the Chinese People's Liberation Army was brutally overthrowing our unique Buddhist culture and bringing us the 'gift' of Communism. I emerged from my mother's womb into the most turbulent, tragic time in Tibetan history. The Chinese had invaded in 1950, spurred on by the revolutionary zeal of Mao Zedong, to rid us, they said, of 'the poison of religion', our 'feudal backward ways'.

The process had started quietly enough but by the time I came along it had gathered momentum and they were in the throes of tearing down our ancient monasteries, turning our sacred Buddhist texts into toilet paper, grinding our ritual implements into paving stones and imprisoning, torturing and killing thousands of our monks, nuns, and anyone who stood in their way. Fear and terror stalked every corner of my land.

Although they insisted Tibet was part of 'The Motherland', the Chinese who so abruptly appeared in our midst were nothing like us. They looked different, smelt different, spoke a different language, ate different food, and most crucially, nurtured a radically different ideology. They had been indoctrinated to believe human beings were primarily socio-economic units useful for bringing about a successful, materialistic society. To Tibetans humankind, and indeed all living things, are essentially holy and are on this earth to perfect their spiritual nature. The clash was inevitable, resulting in horrible displacement and widespread mayhem. This was the background that shaped the course of my childhood and set in motion all the events that followed.

Compounding my precarious beginnings, I was born into a noble family, which to the Chinese class came only second to religion in the evils to be eliminated. On my mother's side, my family was descended from a dual line of aristocracy (although I did not know the details until much later as no one dared speak of such things). One ancestor, Dharmo Menrampa Lobsang Chodak, who was born in the lineage of the royal Tibetan queen Yudra Nyingpo in the Earth Tiger year (1638), was the renowned personal physician to the Fifth Dalai Lama, known as the Great Fifth, the greatest Dalai Lama Tibet has ever known apart from the present one. Like Leonardo da Vinci, he perfected his understanding of human anatomy and physiology by dissecting dead bodies. He was extremely famous, gathered many disciples and wrote several seminal works expounding his findings and healing techniques. Until the Chinese confiscated it, our family possessed the Great Fifth's hat, a prized possession regarded almost as a relic.

We could also trace our line back to Yongzin Pandita Yeshe Gyaltsen, born in the Water Snake year (1713), who became the tutor to the Eighth Dalai Lama. He had three sisters, one of whom married into our family. The Dalai Lama's tutors are not mere teachers, but highly accomplished, revered spiritual practitioners in their own right, and they exercised enormous spiritual and political sway.

My mother, Pema Norzin, was beautiful, with a round face and black lustrous hair that reached below her knees. She was renowned for her unusual, exquisitely shaped eyes – she was nicknamed 'Bright Eyes' – and had many admirers. A warm, kind woman, she was quiet, refined and dignified (unlike me) as befitted her class, and I remember her often telling me to be more demure. I was her third child and first surviving daughter, and I adored her.

Before I arrived my mother had given birth to a girl with a missing thumb on her right hand, who had died when she was one month old. Strangely, shortly after, my aunt had a daughter who also had a missing right thumb. That child died too, this time from the effects of the chemicals, introduced by the Chinese, which were used on their land. Then my mother had a dream in which she saw herself giving birth to a daughter, identical to the other two girls but with all her digits intact. A few months later this was exactly what happened. When I was a toddler my mother would catch me by my thumb, smile and say, 'You were reincarnated three times!' She breast-fed me until I was four and so the bond between us was especially close. When I was around six my mother had another son and years later a second daughter, but I hardly knew them. By that time I was separated from my family and in a place far away.

My father, Wangdu, was completely different, highly strung and often frightening to me. He used to throw things at us when we annoyed him, although none of them actually hit us. It was his way of disciplining us. As my mother was soft, so my father was strict. When we heard him coming home we used to stop playing, rush inside and sit silent, upright and motionless on the benches placed around the sitting room, looking like a still–life picture. I never really knew him and can't recall ever having a proper conversation with him, which now saddens me greatly.

My father was a highly educated, spiritual man who had become a monk aged seven at the historic Riwo Choling monastery in the Yarlung Valley, founded in 1420 by a disciple of Lama Tsong Khapa, the great reformer of Tibetan Buddhism. The Riwo Choling monastery was a complex so vast it covered 50,000 square metres. There my father had received the typical Tibetan monastic education, becoming well versed not only in profound Buddhist philosophy, the art of meditation and the skills of logic, debating, metaphysics, ontology, epistemology, astrology, and medicine, but also in poetry, dancing, painting and music. He played the Tibetan saxophone beautifully and made all of my mother's clothes and shoes.

As a small child I did not realise how much Father had been through. In their general destruction of the monasteries and all things religious, the Chinese had forced him to de-robe, renounce his monk's vows and watch while they systematically pulled down the magnificent Riwo Choling brick by brick, smashing the Buddha statues and riddling the ancient frescoes with bullets. I can see now that it must have been highly traumatic for a man intent on dedicating his life to attaining enlightenment and it probably accounted for his nervous disposition. Shortly after this calamity he had met my mother during the New Year celebrations. They fell in love and remained happily married all their life.

The rest of our household was made up of my two uncles, their wives and 11 children, along with my maternal grandparents. It was a typical Tibetan extended family, full of noise, bustle and human contact. My grandparents were wonderful people and extremely patient with all us children constantly clambering all over them and regaling them with our impromptu plays and concerts. Grandfather had long white hair that my grandmother used to wash and put into plaits. He had once been extremely wealthy and much respected, having owned a monastery outside Lhasa, the capital. But like the rest of the family my grandparents had fallen on hard times. Grandfather was utterly devoted to his wife and used to follow her everywhere. If Grandmother went to the toilet he used to go looking for her.

Grandmother herself was a great matriarch who had given birth to 18 children, 11 of whom had survived. Big families were common in Tibet, before the Chinese came. Of course we did not have contraception, and besides, Tibetans believe in leaving everything to nature. Infant mortality was high – only the toughest children survived. My grandmother was particularly attached to my mother, and would not part with her when she was offered a chance to be educated in Shanghai. As a consequence my mother was illiterate. Grandmother did everything about the house – cooking, sweeping, and cleaning the cooking pots. This must have been hard – when she had been reared there were servants to do all the manual work. But she never complained.

Grandmother could have had several husbands, as polyandry was well established in Tibet, but she chose only my grandfather. We Tibetan women are feisty, bold, strong, earthy creatures, given to flirting and laughing out loud. It's not unknown for Tibetan women to chase men, *and* pinch their bottoms. (My mother, being aristocratic, was an exception!) We're also highly independent and have equal rights both in the home and in business. This independence my mother approved of: 'Soname, make sure you cannot cook. Then your husband will love you for yourself,' she used to say. It was a lesson I learnt well – maybe too well, as over the years it has got me into more scrapes than even I could have imagined.

With such strong connections to two Dalai Lamas my family had been extremely wealthy, by Tibetan standards. We owned a lot of land in Yarlung, large herds of yak and cattle, and kept many servants who worked both in the house and on the land. There were also fine carpets, antique furniture and beautiful turquoise, coral and amber jewellery which my mother and grandmother would wear in their hair as well as around their necks. Tibetan women wear all their jewellery all the time to enhance their beauty as well as for status. But by the time I came along it had all been taken away – apart from one exquisite piece of silk cloth embroidered with honeysuckle flowers, which had mysteriously survived the plunder – and we were dirt poor. And so I experienced nothing of my family's former grandeur, status and power.

Somehow our house had escaped destruction – at least for the time being. To my childish eyes it was magical, even though it had been stripped bare. It stood by itself amid a grove of trees by a small lake and it was huge, consisting of some 15 rooms built on two levels. If you climbed on to the flat roof you could see the mountains of Samye, the site where the very first Buddhist monastery was built. Our house was constructed in a square around an inner courtyard, which was open to the skies. The outer mud walls were a rich red-brown and around the windows were painted bands of gold, blue, red and black in the traditional style. Inside the floors were made of some dark, shiny stone, which was something of a status symbol, since the rest of the village houses had floors only of compacted earth. And halfway up the interior walls were painted bands of bright colour. The whole family lived together in this big house, in winter sharing the downstairs rooms with the yaks and donkeys that had been brought in out of the piercing cold.

The general meeting place was the outside terrace where in summer we would all gather to drink tea, chat and share our meals. In winter we would crowd into the dark, atmospheric kitchen lit only by oil lamps and infused with the grime and smell of years of wood smoke, juniper incense and the butter that we used in all our cooking – including our tea. Tibetans love butter and think it is the cure for everything. It certainly helped keep out the cold by giving us an extra layer of fat. (Electricity did not arrive in our village until 1981, when we were forced to pay for it in chickens and eggs. However, the supply was very weak and you never knew whether it would be working or not, and so my father declared we were better off without it and snipped the wires. The rest of the village followed suit.)

In that kitchen we would huddle around the big earthenware stove, our only source of heat, on which grandmother would be cooking us noodle stew while she told us stories. She would tell us old Tibetan fairy tales so vivid that listening to them was like watching a movie, and she would accompany them with songs. Grandmother had no teeth, but her voice was haunting and beautiful. I loved the songs and knew them all by heart. Grandfather's speciality was ghost stories about demons so petrifying that I would be too scared to go outside to pee, and would insist my parents and my brothers came with me.

On those long winter nights I would bed down in the kitchen, on a mattress my father had made from straw, and cover myself with a quilt that he had sewn from whatever scraps of material he could find. I remember my parents' blankets being woefully thin and threadbare – I don't know how they survived the winter temperatures. When the summer came, however, I would drag my mattress out into the courtyard and sleep under a myriad of stars sparkling like diamonds in a velvet-black sky.

Yarlung Valley, where I grew up, was the cradle of Tibetan civilisation and the home of the first Tibetan kings. You could climb from the valley to the cave on Crystal Mountain where, legend had it, the god of compassion had taken the form of a monkey to mate with a white ogress to create the Tibetan race. The story goes that the god of compassion, who of course was contemplative and peaceful, had heard the plaintive cries of the ogress, who was wrathful with an insatiable sexual appetite. She was lonely and wanted a mate. Out of pity the god of compassion transformed himself into a monkey, went to her, and from their union came six children, the first Tibetans. In the cave you could still see an image of a monkey painted on the wall. By 127 BC the first Tibetan king, Nyatri Tsenpo, had made his home in the Yarlung Valley. Forty-one monarchs followed, reigning in Yarlung for a total of one thousand years. After them came the

Dalai Lamas, spiritual and temporal leaders combined.

Living on the rooftop of the world my playground was spectacular. That awesome, untamed landscape shaped my soul, as it did the soul of every Tibetan, and fostered in me a love of nature and freedom that has never left me. The Yarlung Valley was astonishingly beautiful, surrounded by huge mountains, some 20,000 feet high, and filled with patchwork fields and groves of trees. The valley was divided by the Tsangpo and Chongye Rivers. Yarlung had the best soil in the whole of Tibet. The small lake outside our house provided water for the household, fields and animals. I used to love washing my face in its cool, fresh water.

Our weather was as wild as our landscape. There were fierce storms that threw down hailstones as big as golf balls, ferocious dust storms that lasted days at a time. All we could do was take shelter and ride them out. I heard that two monks once managed to escape from Lhasa because they were buried alive by dust in a storm while working on a prison road gang. They found hollow stems to breathe through and when it was dark they made their getaway.

My ear was tuned to the music of nature since I was young. I was infused with the sound of the mighty wind, the call of the birds, the rushing waters of the rivers in full flood, the sound of the ice squeaking and breaking. There was no traffic and no planes when I was growing up – the only industrial noise was the farmer singing to his yak. (Yaks love to be sung to.) The skies were vast and extraordinary. Everywhere you looked the horizon seemed to stretch into infinity, leading your mind upwards and outwards, instilling you with a sense of infinite space. The sun shone in a cloudless sky so blue it looked purple. This brilliant sun gave us bright red cheeks (and for the unfortunate, cataracts). And the air, like the water, was pure and sparkling, as if it had been created just yesterday.

Being a farming family, our year had its set rhythms. After the long, hard winter we began to emerge outside to work the land. February was ploughing season and also the festival for the yaks and cows. We used to paint their horns, hang bells and ribbon from their long shaggy coats, and feed them the best food we had. This was our way of honouring them and it also helped make them fit for working. All the farms would come together and sit around a big fire in the evening. There would be singing and dancing and a lot of *chang*, our very strong local beer, would be consumed. Any lamas who were around would be invited to bless the fields and the animals. May brought Saka Dawa, the high point of the Buddhist calendar, when we commemorated the Buddha's enlightenment, birthday and death, all rolled into one. Before the Chinese occupation the celebrations would last for 15 days, when everyone would get up before dawn to visit every house in the neighbourhood, drink *chang*, and eat specially cooked biscuits made of woven dough. There would be horse racing, dancing and picnics, which might last for days on end. In my childhood, however, our celebration was restricted to five days and was closely supervised by the Chinese army.

August brought another festival, this time for blessing the fields before the harvest. Sometimes we were shown Chinese films of the war between China and Japan (in which China always won), or Western movies dubbed into Chinese, carefully chosen to reveal the poverty and decadence of the West. 'You see how free and equal you all are now. You could never want to go back to the old system,' they told us. At other times one of the villages would put on a concert or play, and people would come from all around, walking for hours to attend. No one was paid, and entry was free.

September was harvest time when once again all the farms pooled resources. By October all the work was finished, and we could relax. This was when any building work was done – before the winter set in and we were forced indoors for three whole months.

Another event remains firmly lodged in my memory. When I was around three or four years old, everyone had to assemble together one day and cry. To my very young mind this was silly, because as far as I could see no one was hurt. Yet everyone

wailed and made a great deal of noise. When I was older I discovered that Mao Zedong had died and we were all supposed to
mourn on that day. Grandmother told me she had put spittle on
her eyes to make out they were wet with tears.

I was a wild child, high-spirited and most definitely a
tomboy. I spent my days running in the fields, climbing trees,
jumping from high walls. With my brothers I rode squealing
pigs, clutching their coarse wiry hair. We were always up to mis-
chief. I remember catching frogs, putting straws up their bottoms and blowing them up – and then squeezing them until the
spawn came out. Now, every day in my prayers I have to purify
that transgression. We also caught flies and killed them, until
Grandmother told us that flies were mothers too who had
children to look after.

As poor children with no toys, we made our own fun. We
spent hours playing in the rooms where the ornaments and tassels used to decorate the yaks' horns and hair were kept. My
brother was very creative and devised a way of making films. He
would put a puppet up at the mirror, point the mirror so the sun
was shining on it and project the shadow on the wall. The village children couldn't figure it out at all. Sometimes they would
ask him to put on his show at night and never understood why
he would not do it.

As for me, my great passion was singing. I loved to sing. I used
to perform all the time for my family, dressing up in tea towels
and putting on my face the red dye used to stain the yaks' horns.
It would take three days to come off. I often yearned to perform
in the village festivals but my father forbade me, saying that to
be a public performer was lower class – worse than being a prostitute or a performing monkey. Nevertheless my grandmother,
who taught me the old traditional songs of Tibet, predicted that
one day I would be a singer.

How could I know then, as a little girl, how true my grandmother's words were? That my voice would one day be heard far
beyond the Yarlung Valley on the world's stage, and that people
everywhere would be enthralled by the mysterious beautiful

land that I had come from. I was an ordinary Tibetan girl caught up in extraordinary times which would propel me into hair-raising adventures that even I, with my vivid imagination and feisty spirit, could never have dreamt of.

CHAPTER TWO

Dark Times

THE TIBET I NEVER KNEW – the Tibet I had missed only by a few short years – had been extraordinary. A land as rich and rare as Ancient Egypt, with a culture steeped in advanced and esoteric spirituality. It was also a highly secret place. No foreigner was allowed to set foot on its sacred soil and woe betide any outsider who caught a glimpse of the 'Forbidden City', Lhasa. What we were so jealously guarding was, of course, our religion. It was far too precious to risk being exposed to 'barbarians'. Locked behind its icy fortress of the impenetrable Himalayas, my country had become known as the land of magic and mystery. Amazing legends abounded. In Tibet, it was whispered, lamas could fly, could walk through walls, could conjure up demons and spirits at will, could dry wet sheets draped around their bodies while sitting in the snow by raising their 'inner heat', could bring down deadly hailstorms, could live on air alone. In Tibet, rumour had it, you could find the hidden kingdom of Shambhala, if you could discover the secret entrance concealed in some mighty mountainside.

And some of it was true! My country *had* produced many yogis and lamas who could do the most amazing feats – the by-product of their meditation. For the average Tibetan, however, religion was a more simple and earthy affair. Basic, heartfelt faith was the order of the day. My grandparents and all the local villagers kept their spiritual practices to asking the local lama to heal their sick yak and bring about bountiful harvests, and saying prayers over their deceased loved ones in order to help them on to a favourable rebirth. Even though we did have over 6,000 monasteries producing an exceptional number of scholar–saints, the ordinary Tibetan, who was illiterate, knew only how to say mantras, turn prayer wheels, do prostrations in front of sacred images and go on pilgrimages. All of which were regarded as great fun! And for all the holy beings living in caves, it has to be said that Tibet had its rogues, thieves and murderers too.

Whether you were a peasant or a saint, it was the Dalai Lama who held Tibet together. In the old days, before I was born, every Tibetan had total unquestioning devotion to the man they regarded as the living Buddha of Compassion. His status was unique. The Dalai Lama, prime spiritual and temporal leader of all Tibet, could trace his incarnations back in an unbroken lineage to 1391. Each time a Dalai Lama died, the seers and oracles would look for signs pointing out where he was going to be reborn. Then search parties would spread out all over the land looking for the right candidate. When they found him, they would subject him to a number of tests, and when he passed he would be reinstated on the lion throne in the magnificent Potala Palace in Lhasa and given the names The Lotus Thunderbolt, Great Precious Prince of the Soft Voice, Mighty in Speech, Excellent of Knowledge, Absolute in Wisdom, Holder of the Doctrine, The One Without Equal, Powerful Ruler of Three Worlds, and Ocean-Wise. Most people, however, just called him *Kundun*, meaning The Presence.

As a child I knew nothing of the Dalai Lama – I did not even know he existed. He had gone into exile in 1959, 14 years before I was born, taking 100,000 refugees with him. He'd tried to cooperate with the Chinese, but as the oppression increased, and his life was in danger, he had fled over the mountains to India disguised in layman's clothes. He had hoped that by going to

India he could rally international support for his beleaguered country. To no avail. After his departure Tibet fell into an even greater depression. It was as though the final flickering of the last butter lamp had been extinguished. Now, no one dared say his name for fear of being imprisoned and having their tongue torn out. But I think my grandmother had a picture of him hidden under her pillow, which she used to direct her silent prayers to.

I was a happy child, lucky to be born to a loving family in an indescribably beautiful country where I could roam free, but my childhood memories are tainted by the pain I felt witnessing my family's suffering. As a noble family we had all been 'born guilty'. We thus became targets of persecution, both by the Chinese and some of the local people who had been indoctrinated against us, the privileged upper classes. Some were all too keen to get their revenge on the family who had once been their masters.

It was a frightening world and the whole family lived in a constant state of tension. There were knocks on the door at night from villagers sent to spy on us in case we were eating better food than we should be. They would come and stir our meal to see if there was any meat in it. They checked to see that our clothes were patched, a sign that we had become equal with them. We were never allowed to wear anything new. They monitored our conversations to make sure we were toeing the party line and not doing anything subversive, such as praying.

As children, my brothers and I were also given a tough time. We were kicked and punched when we passed and people used to call us bastards – the worst insult a Tibetan could utter. 'Bastard' became almost my second name. In one particularly traumatic incident, my younger brother came home one day distraught. He told us that other children had held him down on the ground and peed into his mouth. My older brother went crazy. Mother begged him to keep calm but he stormed out of the house and went looking to fight the boys who had done it.

Later that night a gang of boys came to our house and broke all our windows. My parents reported the incident to the local committee. Everyone was summoned to attend – and they found our family guilty. My parents were publicly beaten while we all had to watch. I shook with fear. Grandfather had his head held over smoking red-hot chillies, which was excruciatingly painful. It was terrible to see. His face swelled up in huge red welts and he was blinded for days.

Later that year the Chinese authorities accused him of hiding family jewellery on the mountain. It wasn't true, although many Tibetans *did* throw their jewellery into rivers, preferring to return it to a natural source rather than hand it over to the authorities. But Grandfather was locked up for three weeks in an underground store room on our property. My mother used to sneak food and snuff to him in the middle of the night, goodness knows how.

Grandmother had not been spared either. Just before I was born she was forced to join a road gang building canals and roads and made to wade through icy streams all day carrying heavy stones on her back. She developed terrible chilblains and a horrible growth on her spine. Eventually, when she was no longer able to walk, my grandfather put her on a horse and led her to a hospital. She somehow recovered and was allowed to stay at home to look after us. My uncle was also jailed for several years because someone had heard him singing 'Chairman Mao eats shit' on the mountain. He learned to knit in prison and used this skill after he was released to feed his family.

The bane of my parents' life, however, were the 'special meetings for social reform'. These were political gatherings, held at night, at which people of our class were interrogated by committees about their personal history. Their stories were then read to the meeting for criticism and evaluation. Any excuse for public humiliation was found.

One night after 9 pm my mother was summoned to such a meeting. A sixth sense told her to bring my elder brother with her. When they arrived no one was there but a lone Tibetan man who had been eyeing her up. Only my brother's presence saved her from being raped, something that was happening to women everywhere. In one town the women and girls of 400 families were marched naked in public, tortured and raped. It was truly an insane period, like Nazi Germany, when people behaved in the strangest ways and did things they would never normally do. Everyone had been brutalised by Mao's monstrous regime.

My parents' life was excruciatingly hard. Every day they worked in the fields, alongside most people in our village aged between seven and eighty. Their day started at 5 am and ended at 8 pm or 10 pm, depending on the season. The work was backbreaking and many villagers died from exhaustion. Because my mother was breast-feeding me she was allowed an extra half-hour in the morning and evening to look after me, while my grandmother gave me her empty breast for the rest of the day to comfort me. People didn't get wages as such, but were paid in grain rations. Once a year they were each allotted a certain amount, but it was never enough to last.

My parents, like all Tibetans, were hungry a lot of the time. In fact, in the year I was born they nearly starved. Tibet suffered an enormous famine that year, in which tens of thousands perished because China was sending our grain back to feed its own starving millions, who were enduring their own self-imposed famine. Tibet had never experienced a famine before: we knew how to manage our fragile eco-system. But the Chinese prevented us from practising crop rotation, and the results were disastrous.

For all the trauma and poverty, my family (and indeed most of Tibet) coped remarkably well. I can recall times of serenity and even laughter at home. We are by nature a strong, resilient race, with a terrific sense of humour. We love to joke and send each other up, even our lamas – and this helped enormously in those terrible times. And I can honestly say I do not remember any bitterness or resentment in either my family or my fellow countrymen and women. There was just great sadness.

More than anything else, however, it was our faith that kept us going. Nothing, not even the fanatical, destructive rage of the invading Chinese, could take away our sense of the divine and the deepest principles of Buddhism. We had been taught to have compassion towards all, especially our enemies. Now was the time to practise forgiveness. If we retaliated with hostility we knew the enmity would have no end. The Buddha said that anger cannot be overcome with more anger – it can only be quelled with patience and love.

We understood too that everything in life is impermanent and in a constant state of flux. Bad times become good times and vice versa. And we had been taught to be calm in the face of adversity, to try and move beyond emotions, especially negative, destructive ones. I don't mean we never had feelings, quite the contrary – but feelings are different from emotions. We also believed that the Chinese were accruing terrible karma for themselves by creating so much suffering, and they would one day have to suffer in return. You had to feel compassion towards them for that. I will say, however, that it was sometimes hard to be kind, especially when they did not change.

The country had been warned, both by various oracles and the last Dalai Lama, that a terrible event was going to hit Tibet, and so we were halfway prepared. Just before the Thirteenth Dalai Lama died in 1939 he had predicted:

'It may happen, that here, in the centre of Tibet, religion and government will be attacked both from without and from within. Unless we can guard our own country, it will now happen that the Dalai and Panchen Lamas, the Father and Son, and all the revered holders of the Faith, will disappear and become nameless. Monks and their monasteries will be destroyed. The rule of law will be weakened. The lands and property of government officials will be seized. They themselves will be forced to serve their enemies or wander the country like beggars. All beings will be sunk in great hardship and overpowering fear; the days and nights will drag on slowly in suffering.'

Many physical portents just before the invasion had backed up the Dalai Lama's dreadful vision. A bright horse-tailed comet had hung in the sky day and night for many weeks. This was followed by a huge earthquake, felt as far away as Calcutta. Apparently, the whole of south-eastern Tibet glowed with a terrible light and a pungent smell of sulphur filled the air. People said it was like the end of the world. These warnings helped mitigate the pain, a little. Tibet has its own karma too.

However, I thought my life in Yarlung would go on for ever. Then one day when I was nearly seven my mother summoned me and told me to sit down because she had something important to tell me. There was an expression of concern in her eyes. She said it had been decided to send me to Lhasa, the capital, to live with an aunt. It was for my own good, she explained. If I stayed I would soon be forced to work in the fields all day as my parents did and they wanted to spare me such horrible manual labour. They were also concerned for my physical safety. Many young girls were being raped, and I was already vulnerable because of my privileged background.

I did not know it then, but many of us country girls were being sent to the cities in the hope of a better life. In Lhasa, my parents thought, I would have prospects. My aunt worked in a theatre school which might offer me a place to study. Or I might get a proper education at a government school and make something of my life.

I didn't know what to think. As a child I didn't understand the exact meaning of my mother's words. She loved me and I trusted her completely, but I was apprehensive about leaving my family and everything I knew. I had only met this aunt twice and had found her to be rather cold. I had no idea where Lhasa was. Though bold, I was an obedient child. In Tibet we are brought up to obey our parents implicitly. As children we are given no choice and we never answer back.

I was also curious about what I would find in Lhasa. And so I didn't resist. Little did I realise, but from that day on I would never be a child again.

CHAPTER THREE

Slavery

MY AUNT WAS A young woman aged about 26 who lived with her husband, a postman, and two young sons in a little house down a side street not far from the centre of Lhasa. It seemed terribly cramped in comparison to my splendid, rambling home in Yarlung. Dolga, as she was called, was extremely beautiful and a professional dancer and opera singer. She had left Yarlung aged 13, having been chosen by the Chinese Dancing Committee and trained at the Performing Arts College in Lhasa. Every town and village had a representative at the college and she gained a complete education there.

Dolga, who had never been close to the family since she left, was kind but distant. I suspect she wanted to toughen me up and train me not to be homesick, but it didn't work. I missed my family horribly, especially my mother. I was a little girl who had never stood on her own two feet. Until the day I left, my mother was still tying my shoelaces and the belt worn around my traditional long dress, the *chuba*.

Every morning I announced I was going home. 'Your parents are coming for you soon,' my aunt replied. But they never did. She was just trying to placate me, hoping that I'd settle down and forget Yarlung. I played with her sons a little, and that helped distract me, but at night it was awful. My homesickness rose to the surface and I would sob my heart out under the bedclothes so that no one would know. I was a private little girl, who never wanted anyone to see how lost and lonely I was.

The first weeks in Lhasa went by in a complete blur. I was dazed and confused at finding myself in this utterly alien environment. The mountains, fields, streams and vast open skies that I knew and loved now gave way to city streets, noise, cement, thousands of people and, most extraordinary of all, masses of army trucks, buses and motor cars. We hardly ever saw vehicles of any type in Yarlung, but here in Lhasa they were everywhere, belching out disgusting, smelly black smoke. It was so different from the fresh, clean air that I was used to.

My aunt did not take me out much but I do remember that shortly after I arrived we went to see the famous Potala Palace, built by the Great Fifth. The Dalai Lama and his previous incarnations had lived there for hundreds of years, and so had my ancestors. Throughout my childhood Grandmother had regaled me with the story of her one and only visit to the Potala. She would relate in vivid detail how she had seen an extraordinary, enormous, weird animal called an elephant use its long nose to suck up water, then spray it out three times in homage to the Buddha before drinking it. The elephant had been a gift to the Dalai Lama from some Indian prince. I couldn't wait to see this miracle for myself. When I arrived I looked eagerly about, but there was no elephant in sight.

The Potala itself, though, was awesome. I looked up and up and could hardly believe my eyes. Never in my life had I seen anything so big, grand and wonderful. The palace sits on a hill, completely dominating Lhasa; it has 1,000 rooms, and a huge flight of 2,000 stone steps leads up to it. My aunt told me to look carefully. At first glance, she said, it appears completely symmetrical, but if you inspect it closely you can see that the north and east wings are actually of different design. The Chinese had demolished many of our traditional houses in Lhasa and had put up hideous concrete blocks painted apple

green and baby pink in their place, but they had not dared touch
the Potala. Even they recognised it was an architectural master-
piece; it was called by some the eighth wonder of the world.

One day my aunt dressed me in my best clothes and took me
to the Performing Arts College for an audition, as she had
promised my parents. I stood very straight and sang the best I
could. There was a little applause and I was told I'd done very
well. Then they took me away and measured me – my height,
my width, the distance between my ankles and knees, my knees
and hips, and the length of my spine. That was my downfall.
They announced quite brutally that even though my voice was
good, and I met the required standard of physical attractiveness,
they had calculated I was not going to reach the required height
for a singer. I was going to be too small. In hindsight this was
ridiculous, but under Communism everything was dictated by
rules, including the creative arts. 'Maybe you can become an
office worker,' my aunt said vaguely. I nodded, although I had no
idea what an office girl did.

Two months after the audition my aunt told me that I could
no longer stay with her and she was sending me to her husband's
brother's place. I suppose they didn't know what to do with me.
The people I was to live with were called Mr and Mrs Tashi, she
explained, and they needed someone to keep house for them
while they were both out at work. My uncle had driven his
postal van to Yarlung to discuss this proposition with my parents
and they had approved. They still felt that I would have a better,
safer life in Lhasa, even though they were missing me.

'When they go out to work you shut the door, and don't
open it again until they come back,' my aunt instructed. What
could I do? I was only a child and had no choice. I was taken
to this new family holding an apple in my hand, but I never
ate it. My stomach was too tight with apprehension and
homesickness.

The Tashis lived not far away and we were able to walk there.
While I stood trembling inside with trepidation, my aunt
knocked on their door. It was opened by Mr Tashi, who ushered

us in and introduced me to the family. I saw a tall, nice-looking couple aged somewhere in their thirties. They told me that they both had very busy, important jobs working for the Police Department, which like all government departments was run from Beijing, and that they badly needed help with the house-keeping. I was going to be trained to do all the housework, shopping and washing for the whole family. There was a son, Dawo, who was my age, a younger daughter, Tsering, who was a weekly boarder and only came home at weekends, and two Lhasa Apso dogs.

The house was small by comparison to my own home but infinitely more comfortable. I noticed lots of good furniture, ornaments and Tibetan rugs of high quality. The Tashis clearly had no money worries. There were two bedrooms, a sitting room, a kitchen and a small garden. My aunt kissed me good-bye, told me to be good and left. The last tenuous link with my family was severed – I felt more lost and alone than ever.

I stood there, saying nothing, not knowing what to do. 'You can put your things in the shed in the garden, and at night you will roll a mattress out on the kitchen floor and sleep there,' Mr Tashi told me. At least that part of my new life was going to be familiar, I thought. My Cinderella life had begun. It was to con-tinue unabated for almost ten years.

It started off easily enough. For the first few months Mr Tashi's father came to stay to instruct me in the lighter chores – sweeping, dusting and polishing – and watch over me to make sure I did nothing wrong. When he was confident I knew my duties he returned to his home and left me to it. Then the work became harder and longer. I had been conscripted.

My daily routine is etched indelibly in my mind. How could it be otherwise when I performed it seven days a week for ten long years? I got up at 6 am, before sunrise, and emptied the family's chamber pots. Then followed a whole list of chores while the family were still in bed – watering the plants, raking and then making the fire (using dried yak dung as fuel), polish-ing the bicycles – including the spokes – and churning the but-

ter tea which had to be kept hot all day, without curdling, ready
to serve. Even the simple task of boiling water was an epic task
in Tibet because at that altitude, in such thin air, liquid takes
hours to come to the boil. Luckily I never had to prepare breakfast or any other meal because the Tashis were too afraid I would
burn the place down. Mother would approve of that, I thought.
After breakfast I had to comb Mrs Tashi's hair, massage her scalp,
and pull out any grey hairs I found.

When they had left for work I set about the major housework: dusting, making their beds, oiling and then shining the
wooden floors, polishing all the big brass cooking pots, heir-
looms passed down by Mrs Tashi's mother who used to brew
chang in them. I was always terrified I'd drop one and dent it.
Sweeping was really hard work because they insisted I move all
the heavy furniture to get up every little speck of dirt. Those
Lhasa Apsos drove me mad as they left their hair everywhere.
But from all this hard physical work I became extremely strong.
Before too long I could even take their rugs down to the river
on a bicycle to wash and bring them back wet and doubly
heavy, which was a real balancing act. I may have been small but
I could lift a 50-kilogram sack of rice.

The chores went on all day, though there was a break for
lunch when the Tashis came home. We'd eat together; at least
they were not stingy with food, and I ate rather a lot, becoming
quite plump. I couldn't believe there was so much food after the
shortages in the countryside.

There was shopping to do in the Barkhor, the market that
surrounds Lhasa's central temple, the Jokhang. The first time I'd
gone there, clutching coins to buy spring onions for the family's
lunch of *mo-mos* (dumplings), I had become so absorbed in the
bustle and fascinating sights that I completely lost track of the
time and didn't arrive back until evening – still clutching the
coins. The Tashis were furious. After that, I was never allowed
out without permission.

In the afternoon I was left alone with the family's washing.
This was the worst job of all. Of course, there were no washing

machines in Tibet then, which meant I had to scrub all the clothes by hand in the yard. It was gruelling work for small hands, particularly when jeans came to Tibet, a few years later. Washing jeans by hand is like washing leather, they become stiff and hard. I hated those jeans! Rinsing in cold water was no fun either, especially in winter, when the water was icy cold. I never dared stop or run inside to warm my hands around a cup of tea, because if I did, by the time I got back, the clothes would be too frozen to hang up. I gritted my teeth and battled on. Very quickly my hands soon stopped looking like a child's, they looked as if they belonged to a farmer – all red and swollen. I dreaded the weekends even more, when the daughter came home and relatives visited, adding their laundry to the pile. It would have helped if they had said 'I hope you don't mind,' but they never did.

The drudgery went on all day and much of the night too. There was always washing up after dinner, shoes to shine, wood to chop for the fire, clothes to mend, food sacks to wash and darn after the mice had been at them. I often did not roll out my mattress on the kitchen floor until 11 pm, and I would fall asleep immediately, completely exhausted. In the summer, however, I would drag my bedding into the garden so I could look up at my beloved stars and be lulled to sleep by the wind on my face, like I used to do in Yarlung. For a few brief moments I was transported back to the unbounded Tibetan wilderness of my early childhood, when my spirit and my body roamed free. And in the deepest recesses of my mind I touched the happiness I had known then.

Over the years I grew used to being a drudge, working all hours for no money, just my board and keep. Gradually it became the only life I knew. The housework itself, although strenuous and relentless, did not make me unhappy. Tibetans, and I was no exception, are used to working very hard and actually like it. I had watched my parents and countrymen toil incredibly long hours in the fields in rain, blizzards and freezing cold without complaint and I must have inherited their genes, because I have never been lazy. In fact I was a good, conscientious worker and gained quite a reputation among the family's friends and acquaintances. I wanted to do things well.

What was excruciatingly painful, however, was the emotional cruelty. The Tashis never beat me or tortured me, but they starved me completely of love and affection. I was simply a worker to them. They would give their own children sweets, but not me. There were snacks, like biscuits, between meals, but I could not touch them. They would take their children to the cinema, but leave me behind, saying I would not behave well. Sometimes it hurt. When they first got a TV, I eagerly sat down to watch a programme and they told me to get up and stop watching because I would become addicted. I did not dare watch it after that. In such an atmosphere, not surprisingly, I was tense all the time, constantly frightened of doing or saying the wrong thing. Every day I walked on eggshells. I thought that if I continued to work hard and did what I was told, they would show me love, but they never did.

Just as hard as receiving no affection was the fact that I had no one to give my love to. Having no one I could put my arms around, no one to share my feelings with, left a gaping hole inside me. To be able to give love is a great gift. I got on quite well with Dawo, the son, but could never share my thoughts with him because he'd repeat everything to his parents. And Tsering, the daughter, was too young. I remember once playing a stone-throwing game with her. When I won, she ran crying to her mother. After that I always made sure I lost, which was no fun at all.

As bad as the emotional deprivation was the repression. I had no freedom, which was torture for my unbounded spirit. I was forbidden to go anywhere by myself, to open the door to anyone, to talk to any of the neighbours. I was in a virtual prison. Nor was I allowed to make a single decision by myself. They told me when to get up, when to go to bed, what to do with practically every minute of the day and night, and then checked that I had done it properly. They disciplined me all the time. Mrs

Tashi even did my hair for me, which I hated. I wasn't allowed to wear it how I wanted, to experiment with different styles, or to let it just hang loose, which is what I longed to do sometimes. Every day she would plait it in two long straight braids, and that was that. The braiding of my hair became a symbol of my entrapment.

I even had to ask permission to go to the toilet, which was a public one just around the corner. Getting away to that toilet was my one small but guaranteed taste of freedom during the day. When I grew older I used to wake up early and sneak out to clean the toilet. Tibetan public toilets can get pretty disgusting, especially after children have used them. There is no nice clean porcelain bowl, with flushing water and tidy drains to take the waste away. Instead Tibetans are invited to squat over a wooden slit in a pile of planks, and allow their effluent to drop a great distance to a pit far below. Often it's a hit and miss affair – and there are usually faeces and urine all over the floor.

I thought that if I cleaned the toilet and made it pleasant for people to go to, it would be like a purification ritual, to cleanse my negative karma and help me get a better future. Although it was dirty I didn't mind. I'm not squeamish by nature and I felt I'd done something good – making people happy and helping myself at the same time. I discovered that if your intention is pure you don't feel dirty at all.

It was in the toilet that I met my friend Wangmo. A neighbour, she was a year older than me. She too had come from the country to Lhasa, in her case to be a nanny. Poor thing – she was looking after five children and had a huge workload. It helped me to realise that I was not alone in my fate. Many of the young country girls who had been sent to the towns for a better life had ended up as virtual slaves. Wangmo and I used to meet nearly every day in the public toilet, if we could, at 3 pm. We talked about missing our parents, our lives before we came to Lhasa, and the scoldings we were given. We used to share any food we had managed to salvage.

Later it was Wangmo who helped me when my period came.

I didn't know what was happening – I woke up one morning, my bedding all sticky with blood, and thought I was dying. She told me it was OK, that it happened to her every month and I should put newspaper in my pants. This made me quite ill – my face swelled up and I felt giddy. I think the newspaper ink poisoned my system, and after that I used rags. Wangmo was wonderful, my best mate. Without her my life would have been unbearable.

Apart from seeing Wangmo, the other highlight of my day came after I'd finished the laundry, when I rewarded myself by playing music. Music was still my great love, but in this house it was forbidden to me. The Tashis, though, had a stack of Chinese love songs on tape and they sometimes played them in the evening. So I watched very carefully to see how they worked the tape recorder, committing every step to memory. When they were out I put on my favourite numbers, noting the exact place where the tape had been stopped, so they wouldn't suspect. I'd sing along at the top of my voice, karaoke style.

One day the tape broke. I was terrified. I prayed very hard to the Buddha: 'Please help me, Buddha. I promise I'll never touch the tape recorder again!' I did not like to think about what the Tashis would do if they found out. But the Buddha must have heard my prayers because Wangmo had a copy of the very same tape, and she gave it to me. I kept my promise to the Buddha for about a month. Then I cracked. I couldn't live without music. Singing was my passion, my great release from bondage.

A few years on I heard a tape of Michael Jackson, and I thought he was fabulous. It was my first experience of Western music – apart from the crazy road-sweeping vehicles that went up and down the main road squirting water into the gutters while they played Western classical music (I later learnt it was Beethoven's Ninth Symphony). China was trying to make Tibet modern.

By 1982, when I was about nine and had been at the Tashis' for two years, the Cultural Revolution had ended and things began to ease up a little in Tibet. People were allowed to travel more freely within the country and my parents and grandparents paid me a visit in Lhasa. It was truly wonderful to see them but it felt strange saying 'Mother' and 'Father' again – I hadn't said those words for so long. Coming to see how I was, they announced that conditions in the countryside were a little better and that it was probably safe now for me to go home. But the Tashi family begged them to let me stay, saying what a great worker I was and claiming they were going to organise a City ID card for me, which would entitle me to special housing and food benefits when I was older. They said they were in a position to arrange a good marriage for me, and an office job too. They even hinted that one day their house would be mine.

These were enormous hooks, infinitely more than my parents could offer. They thought long and hard about it and then said, 'Our life in Yarlung is pretty difficult. Many of the villagers still give us a hard time because of our former status. You will be better off here.' My heart sank and I clung to my mother's hand. But as always I acquiesced, obeying her completely. It didn't occur to me to be angry or blame her. I assumed she was doing what she thought best for me. In Tibet mothers are universally revered, and so I thought about my mother's wishes more than my own. Maybe she can't look after me, I mused. And then my parents left.

After that, every New Year I would announce to the Tashis that I wanted to go home and join in the family reunion and all the festivities. New Year in Lhasa was particularly hard for me because the Tashis invited many guests, including Chinese, increasing my workload considerably. The Chinese would spit sunflower husks all over the floor, making a terrible mess. 'You can go next year,' or 'You can go for your summer holiday,' the Tashis replied. It never happened. But I kept hoping, and that hope kept me alive.

The slight relaxation in the rules also meant that a few intrepid Westerners began to trickle into Tibet, curious to see for themselves the secrets of our Forbidden Land. I don't know if these visitors found us as fascinating as they hoped, but they were certainly an eye-opener to me. For the first time in my life I saw blond, blue-eyed people, with white eyelashes and red skins. To my eyes they looked extraordinary – like beings from another planet. They were unnaturally big and the men had hair on their arms and legs, which was very weird. It also struck me that their bodies and clothes were all so clean in comparison to ours, and as they walked past they smelt of flowers. It must have been the soap and shampoo they used. No one ever smelt like that in Tibet. Sometimes I would bump into Western women in the toilet and was intrigued by their pretty knickers.

Western touches also began to appear in Lhasa. One day I spotted a gigantic cut-out figure of a Western film star, naked to the waist, wearing a bandana and carrying a huge machine gun, which had been erected at the base of the Potala on top of a café. It was Rambo – and it looked totally incongruous and sacrilegious set against the Dalai Lama's palace. But I suppose that was the effect they wanted to achieve.

The end of the Cultural Revolution also heralded a certain amount of religious tolerance, at least on the surface. People gradually began to go on pilgrimages again and from the talk around the Barkhor, the big market place, I learnt that Tibetans were beginning to walk around the Potala again, in the age-old religious ritual of performing *cora*. I had heard stories of how, at dawn and at sunset, my people would stop what they were doing to walk all the way around a sacred object, be it a temple or a shrine, spinning their hand-held prayer wheels and saying their sacred mantras.

I decided to join in, to see what it was like. One morning I got up very early, around 3 am, crept out of the house and made my way through the back alleys to the foot of the Dalai Lama's palace. There were literally hundreds of people, some with their animals, all walking around the base of the great building, under a vast panoply of stars, moving in a clockwise direction. All you could hear was a great hum, like a million locusts – the sound of the throng muttering the Dalai Lama's mantra of compassion, *om mani padme hum*, which means 'hail to the jewel in the lotus', a metaphor for the compassion that lies within every sentient being. The atmosphere was heavy with reverence and awe. It was unbelievably exciting.

For me the thrill was magnified by the fact that I was out by myself, tasting freedom and breathing in the fresh, chilly air. On that early morning there was so much freedom. I told Wangmo about it, and after that we used to go together as often as we dared. We never got much sleep, but it did not matter at all. These were some of the most enjoyable times of my life in Lhasa.

Somehow, over the years I survived. I got into a rut of work. The sheer discipline of being kept so physically busy, tired from dawn to dusk, kept me going, and stopped me thinking too much. I simply did not have the time to be depressed. But the loneliness was always there. The longing for my home and my family never went away and at moments it was almost unbearable. And almost every night for the first few years, after everyone had gone to bed, I continued to cry under the bedclothes, making sure no one could hear me, just as I did at my aunt's. I never wanted to let the Tashis know how much I was hurting. Eventually I learnt not to have feelings. I became numb, cut off, dead inside. It was easier that way.

Very occasionally I received a letter from my father, saying he hoped I was well and adding that my mother missed me – especially at New Year when she would cry because I was absent from the festivities. And then I would recall her words to me: 'If you stay in the city you won't have to do farm work, you will get an education and make something of your life.' No matter how long I stayed, however, no education was forthcoming, there was no City ID card and no office job. I thought, this is my karma, to be in slavery. Obviously I have to pay back something that I have done in a previous life and I must not complain because I am carving out my future all the time with my present actions.

So I endured, and from hardship I grew strong. As the days, months and years went by, I grew confident in my ability to withstand deprivation and excessively hard situations. It was to hold me in very good stead. They did not intend it, but in fact the Tashis served me well.

CHAPTER FOUR

Running Away

IN ALL THE YEARS I worked for the Tashis I only went back to my home twice. The first time was shortly after my parents and grandparents had come to see me in Lhasa in 1982. I was very unsettled by their visit, unable to get on with the daily chores in the same robotic way. They had stirred up in me emotions and longings that I'd successfully buried for a long time and my dissatisfaction grew.

One day while drying the dishes I broke a glass. When the Tashis came home they were furious and scolded me with a harshness that didn't fit my crime. Nor did they let the matter drop. For days afterwards they kept haranguing me about how clumsy I was, how I wasn't doing my work properly. Suddenly something in me snapped. I'd had enough. I didn't make a scene, I didn't break down – I simply decided to run away, to go back home. Without any further ado, when they were out at work, I walked out of the front door.

I made my way to Sera monastery, where one of my uncles lived. I knew that in performing his duty of hospitality he would spontaneously give me food, which I would need for my journey. Sera, one of the three great monastic universities in Tibet, was about two hours away on the outskirts of Lhasa. It's a huge place consisting of many chapels and colleges, and sits under a mountain with a big, beautiful Buddha painted on it. It used to house 5,000 monks but now only a few hundred remained.

As I expected, my uncle greeted me warmly and handed me some left-over *tsog*, blessed ritual food that has been offered to the Buddha as part of a religious ceremony. It consisted of biscuits and dried fruit. I didn't dare tell him my plan because he would definitely have forbidden it. When I left him it was mid-afternoon. He gave me money and put me on a bus back to Lhasa, but I never got off. I just kept going until the bus reached the end of its journey, far outside the centre of town. From there I set off across the fields, not really knowing where I was going, but led by some primordial homing instinct. I kept walking and walking until it began to get dark.

I was just wondering what I was going to do, whether I was completely crazy setting off into the unknown by myself, when I heard a mechanical sound. I followed it and came across some sort of factory. There seemed to be no one around – the workers must have all gone home. Finding some big empty cardboard boxes stacked outside, I got inside one of them and fell fast asleep. It was a good, dreamless sleep. After all, I was used to sleeping on the floor.

In the early morning I woke up quite refreshed and carried on walking. Coming across a stream, I drank from it, and nibbled on the *tsog*. Later I found a field where radishes were growing, and ate some of those too. I walked for a long time, through field upon field, thinking how glad I was to be away from the Tashis, my mind absolutely set on reaching Yarlung.

As it grew dark on the second night, I looked around to see if I could see any houses or farms, or perhaps another factory, but there was no sign of human habitation. Tibet is a huge country, bigger than Europe, but its population is only six million, and one can walk for days without seeing another living soul. What could I do? I found a potato field, pulled my clothes around me, curled up in one of the furrows and tried to sleep.

I may have been only nine but I was not afraid of being all

alone in the middle of the countryside, in the open, in the dark. In my mind there was nothing to be frightened of. I certainly wasn't afraid of any animals that might be roaming out there in the dark. Most of the wild animals had been hunted nearly to extinction by the Chinese, and I was used to seeing mice and rats in Lhasa. Besides, I was a child of nature. I am never afraid when I am out of doors. And those years of slavery had toughened me up, made me far more resilient than most children my age.

It was midsummer and not very cold. Even so, I woke up several times during the night because I was chilled, and jumped up and down to get warm again before settling back in my furrow to sleep. In the morning I finally woke with dew in my hair. I washed myself in it and continued on my way, skipping along, filled with boundless energy.

I came across a field which looked as if it was sown with beautiful new green grass. When I stepped on to it, however, I rapidly found myself sinking in mud. I think it was rice. Somehow I grabbed hold of some reeds and managed to pull myself out before gingerly retracing my steps. I was safe, but my clothes were filthy and my shoes were completely waterlogged and caked with mud. I took them off, tied the shoelaces around my neck and walked barefoot. There was nobody around, so I took my clothes off at the next stream and washed them, and my shoes too, sitting naked in the sun while they dried.

I lay on the ground and looked up at the clouds scudding across the sky. I listened to the sound of the stream. I watched the dragonflies hovering above the water. I marvelled at the mighty *ghos* (vultures) riding the currents of air above, their huge wings outstretched. I felt the earth beneath my small naked body. I smelt the soil, the scent of crops on the breeze. I was in heaven. To be free in my beloved countryside, surrounded by nature, after years of confinement in that city house, was sheer bliss. In that wide, open, beautiful Tibetan countryside I had at last come home. The peace was indescribable. Time seemed to have stood still and I could have stayed out in those fields for ever.

Eventually, but with no sense of urgency, I set off again. In the distance I saw two children. When they came closer I asked if they knew where Yukoo was. (This was the town on the farthest outskirts of Lhasa where everyone stopped for petrol.) I knew that if I reached Yukoo, it would be easy to get a lift back to my village. They pointed towards the horizon and said Yukoo was miles away. 'I'm not worried,' I replied. 'I'll walk slowly.'

I slept in another potato field and on the following day carried on walking. Quite soon I began to smell petrol fumes and knew that Yukoo could not be far away. The smell grew stronger and stronger as I walked, and suddenly there was the petrol station. I spotted a lorry parked on the side with the name of my village written on it. There was no one in the cab but I got in, sat down on the front seat and waited.

Shortly two men came along, and they were somewhat taken aback to find a small, scruffy girl perched up front behind the steering wheel. Having checked that they were going towards Yarlung, I asked if they could kindly give me a lift as I had no money. 'Why?' they asked. 'I'm going home,' I replied simply. That seemed to satisfy them. 'No problem,' they said. 'Let's get going.' We drove for hours, stopping once when they treated me to tea and a snack. I was rather hungry by then and demolished the food very quickly. The drivers looked at me: 'Poor thing,' they said.

When we were close to Yarlung I asked them to set me down. 'I can find my own way from here,' I said. I didn't want them to know exactly where I lived in case they told the police they had picked up a wandering girl and the Tashis would come and get me. Passing several men and women on bicycles, I walked down the road towards my village.

It was around noon by now and very hot. Remembering that my mother had always told me that upper-class women never exposed their faces to the searing summer sun because it gave them wrinkles, I made myself a hat of leaves to shield my face from the sun. I thought I'd do the job properly and pack mud on my face as well. I felt it would please my mother!

When a jeep came along, I flagged it down, hoping it would give me a lift all the way home. To my horror it was being driven by a Tibetan policeman. 'Where are you headed?' he asked. Because this small road led only to Yarlung, I had no choice but to mention the name of my family. Everyone for miles around knew my family.

'Oh, you belong to them. Jump in,' he said. 'What have you done with your face?' I told him I'd packed it with mud to stop getting sunburnt. 'You kids are devils these days,' he said good-humouredly. I was glad I'd found such a nice policeman. I looked like a beggar-girl by now, and he took me to his own home first so that I could wash my face and generally clean up. His wife gave me some tea before he drove on to my family home.

When I arrived at my house about 5 pm, all the village came out to see what was happening. Police vehicles hardly ever came to Yarlung and they thought some criminal activity was afoot. Then they saw me. 'Yangchen has come back!' they cried.

I walked through the front door of my house. But when my father looked up and saw me he shouted, 'What are you doing here?' He was very angry. 'Don't be so harsh,' my mother retorted quickly, and I ran to her. I think they were both extremely scared because I was with a policeman, and they wondered what I had done. But he was really a very decent man. 'I just found her on the road and thought I'd drop her home,' he said.

It was not the reception I'd expected, longed for. When the policeman left my father went crazy and swore at me. But I told them about the broken glass and the scolding, how I had left because I had had enough. They asked how I had got home, so I recounted the story of my travels. My mother began to cry, but my grandparents laughed: 'This is a very funny monkey!' The tension had been eased considerably.

We went up to the kitchen and sat round the table. The Tibetan tea was poured and we ate *tsampa*, the traditional food made out of roasted barley flour. No Tibetan can live without *tsampa* – it's more than just food to us, it's like divine medicine. I was still famished from my journey, in spite of the snack, and never had *tsampa* tasted so good. 'Are you starving in Lhasa?' my mother asked anxiously. 'No. I don't miss *tsampa*, I miss you,' I replied.

We spent the whole of the first night talking, catching up on the news. The biggest item was that my mother had just given birth to another child – a daughter, called Lakchung Dorga, meaning White Goddess. My father had named her at birth because she was exceptionally beautiful. She had emerged from my mother's womb with a halo of curly hair and red, rosebud lips. In time she became famous throughout the region for her astonishing good looks. I was thrilled to have a sister at last, but we were soon to be separated. It would prove impossible for many years to forge the bond with her that I yearned for.

The following morning my father wrote a letter to the Tashis saying his daughter was safe with her family and for the next week I relived the happiness of my early childhood. I ran and ran in the fields. I played. I snuggled up to my grandmother. Because I was now wearing jeans, rather than the traditional dress, I became a heroine to the village children who had once tormented me on account of my birth. 'You look beautiful,' they cried. They thought I was amazingly modern. I'd also acquired a posh Lhasa accent. I was a city girl. For a few days I felt like a star. I was invited into all the village houses to have tea and coffee and tell them what Lhasa was like. I helped my parents out on the farm as much as I could, washed their clothes and served them tea, hoping this would persuade them to keep me. I was very, very happy.

And then a jeep arrived, sent by the Tashis, to pick me up and bring me back. They sent clothes and sweets and a message that they felt they were missing an arm without me and couldn't manage. 'You are needed, you have to go,' announced my father. My mother said nothing. I don't know why. It was how people were in Tibet at that time. Centuries of feudalism, where no one bucked the system, followed by years of torture and terrorism

from the Chinese during the Cultural Revolution, made everyone bowed and meek. Of course I did not want to go, but I
resigned myself to my karma once more. I tried to be positive.
Maybe I *will* get an education one day, I thought. Maybe the
Tashis, who have influence and are well connected, *will* organise a good marriage for me. Maybe my life *will* improve. Still, I
made the jeep wait three days.

I was taken back to Lhasa, subdued but not beaten. The Tashis
did not scold me now. In fact they were quite civil, for a little
while at least. I think they realised they had gone too far, pushed
me over the edge. I picked up the threads of my humdrum, gruelling existence without complaint, but I was far from happy.

About two years after my great leap of freedom back home I
received one of the rare letters from my father. It announced
that my mother was very ill, and I should come home immediately. My heart stopped, my mind went blank. For my father to
write these words could mean only one thing – that my mother
was dying. The thought was too dreadful to bear. Every fibre of
my being wanted to rush to her side. The Tashis, who had read
the letter to me, could not hold me back. For once, their
humanity came to the fore and they let me go. They even sent
me home in their jeep.

CHAPTER FIVE

Sky Burial

I ARRIVED BACK AT YARLUNG in the early evening, my mouth dry, my heart beating loud enough for the whole village to hear. The first shock that confronted me was completely unexpected – my family house had gone. My magical childhood home with its many rooms, its exquisite painted woodwork, its special shiny, black floor and wonderful upstairs terrace had been demolished. My poor family had been forced to pull it down themselves, brick by brick. The reason they were given was that it had to give way to a road, but the road had never been built. I could hardly imagine how they must have felt, not just at losing their ancestral home but at having to endure yet again being the targets of a painful exercise in public humiliation and spite.

In place of the house they had had to erect a 'modern', soulless, two-roomed concrete box, situated away from the valley at the base of a treeless mountain, and isolated from other houses. I hated it on sight. It was ugly, horrible, cramped, damp and dangerous. When it rained, water gushed down the mountain side and flooded the lower room.

Pushing my horror at the new house to the back of my mind in order to deal with what lay ahead, I opened the door and stepped tentatively inside. I found my mother in bed, with my father, little sister and grandparents nearby. She looked dreadful. Her lovely body had faded away to a skeleton, her long black hair had lost its lustre, her skin was drawn and dry, and the sparkle had gone out of those famed, unusual eyes. It was heart-breaking to behold her.

I could not understand how she could have become like this in the relatively short time since I had seen her. Father explained that she had not been feeling well even when they had visited me in Lhasa, but had no idea what the problem was. She had mentioned nothing to me, he said, because she had not wanted to worry me. That was so typical of her sweet, unselfish nature. On her return to Yarlung she had become much worse, and had gone to a hospital where they had diagnosed an advanced form of stomach cancer. After that she had deteriorated rapidly. 'She kept going until she knew you were coming home – then she took to her bed,' my father added. The light was clearly going out of her and even to my inexperienced gaze she looked like someone not long for this earth.

For the next few days I stayed by her bedside day and night, refusing to leave. I was trying to make up for all the years I had been apart from her, wanting to get as much of her as I could during whatever time she had left. I poured my love on to her, doing everything for her that I could think of. I washed her face, combed her hair, massaged her feet with oil, trying to soothe away her pain. I tried to persuade her to sip a little tea, to eat a little *tsampa*. I even gave her the bedpan. Having emptied the Tashis' bedpans for years and cleaned the public toilet, this was nothing to me. My life had made me stronger and more able to cope than my younger brother and sister, who were going about with scared looks on their faces. I found I could put on a calm, cheerful face in order not to worry or upset her. I may have been only a young girl, but inside I was already an adult.

Mother held on until my oldest brother, who now lived in a town quite far away, came home. When the time came, she took my hand. 'When you are not here I miss you so much,' she whispered. I had waited so long to hear the words from her own mouth rather than from my father's occasional letter. It was a bittersweet moment and had I not adored and revered her as much as I did, I might have been filled with anger and resentment. Then she added, looking right into my eyes with the sweetest expression, 'Don't be too sad.'

It was the last thing she said. I cradled her tiny, thin body in my arms and without fear or revulsion kissed her cold lips, before covering her waxy, still face with a *katag,* a white, ceremonial scarf. 'You are a very good girl. You've done everything possible for your mother,' my father said. I almost detected pride in his voice. It was rare praise indeed.

I did not cry. My tears had been sealed up a long time ago, buried so deep I could not reach them. Still, that did not mean I was not affected. I was far from heartless. Losing your mother is a devastating experience – when you are only 12 how could it be anything else than shattering?

My mother was 49 years old, the most dangerous age of all according to Tibetan tradition, when we believe you are faced with many challenges and your life force can run out. We kept her body in the house for three days, according to custom, putting butter lamps and incense all around it. And we were very careful how we acted and spoke around her because, we believe, she would have been extremely sensitive and clairvoyant at this time, still very much connected to her house and family. We made sure we did not quarrel, say anything negative about her, do anything that would disturb her peace of mind, which was crucial at this stage of her transition. I made sure I kept my mother's cup filled with tea, so that she would know she was still included and loved.

Then we called in a lama to recite to her the Tibetan Book of the Dead, which is what every Tibetan tries to do when someone dies. If possible it's read over a period of 49 days, the time the deceased is in the Bardo, which is what we call the space between lives. The Tibetan Book of the Dead is a very ancient text which comforts and guides the departing person through the rapids of death to his or her next life.

I listened while the lama told my mother not to be confused, that she was now dead and could not linger on here, but was to move forward with confidence. He said she would see many visions, some beautiful and peaceful, others terrifying and wrathful, but whatever appeared she was not to be distracted or caught up in them because they were merely projections of her own mind. 'Keep moving forward fearlessly until you reach the blissful clear light, which signals your true death,' he read. 'Stay in the blissful clear light for as long as you can. This is your true Buddha nature.' Fascinated and entranced, I heard the lama's intonations.

After that, he continued, she would proceed to the Bardo, when her karma would dictate the form and conditions of her next existence. I had no idea where my mother would find herself – only a high lama would be able to tell. She might be reborn in one of the many heavens, or as a human, a bird, a dolphin, an insect, or even (it made me shudder) in hell. It all depends on the purity of your life. Even if you are a strict practitioner and say many prayers it does not mean you will have a good rebirth. The only thing that matters is the true state of your heart and mind. Wherever Mother ended up, however, it would not be permanent – neither heaven nor hell. No life lasts for ever. When the karma of one life runs out, we die, and then start another. In this way we circle around and around on the wheel of life, sampling one type of existence after another, until we have learnt all our karmic lessons and achieve enlightenment.

It never occurred to me to question anything the lama was saying – to me, as for all Buddhists, reincarnation is a fact of life, as inevitable as the seasons. We believe that all living things, humans, animals, insects, birds, fish, as well as beings on other planets and spheres of existence, are made up of two things, body and mind, which we also call consciousness or awareness. These two are connected but very different in nature. The body is physical, the mind is non-physical. All our thoughts, emotions, feelings, perceptions and ideas come under the category of mind

– but mind is infinitely vaster and subtler than that. When we die it is our consciousness, which is non-material, that separates from our body and travels on to its next existence. It's like a snake shedding its skin, or someone getting on a plane to go to another country.

The mind is a very complicated subject and through the centuries Tibetans have studied and written many texts about it. In fact, that is what our Buddhism is about – developing the understanding of our own mind, and evolving it to the state of full awakening or Buddhahood. It is what our entire country was involved in before the Chinese invasion.

As an uneducated girl, of course I knew little about the mind except the simplest facts, like what happens at death. But later I learnt that the mind exists as a stream of consciousness, one moment of awareness leading to another in a continuous line stretching back to what is called 'beginningless time'. That is why reincarnation is possible and how it takes place. When we die our mind goes on, severed from its old body, taking with it all the imprints it has gathered during its life on earth – in other words, its karma. If we have been angry, jealous or aggressive then we have amassed the habits of these harmful, destructive emotions in our mind stream and will draw to ourselves a disturbing and unhappy rebirth. If, on the other hand, we have been gentle, kind and wise, then we will be drawn to a peaceful, happy next life. Karma is all-important – we reap what we have sown. As such, we believe that we ourselves are responsible for the kind of life we have, not any outside god. We literally make our own life. Our external reality reflects our inner reality.

It is said that ordinary people, when they die, have little or no control over their minds because they are so terrified of finding themselves without a fleshly body, and that consequently they are at the mercy of all their mind projections. That is why we read the Tibetan Book of the Dead to them, to help soothe and direct them. Still, they are normally flung into their next birth according to their karma without much say in the matter.

Accomplished meditators, however, who have spent decades looking into their mind and learning how to control it, can do amazing feats at death. There are many stories of lamas who stay sitting bolt upright in the lotus position for days and even weeks after their breath has stopped, with their complexion still fresh and their bodies still pliable. There is no smell of decay about them at all. They are continuing to meditate in the Bardo, using the powerful clear light of mind to dictate whatever future rebirth they want. When their meditation is finished, their body collapses, rigor mortis sets in and they begin to smell like a normal corpse.

More spectacular tales tell of yogis who attain what is known as the 'Rainbow Body' at death, whereby they manage to dissolve all their physical elements into light. When their followers go looking for them they find no sign of a body – only their clothes. Yogis who don't quite reach that exalted level in their death meditation leave behind their nails and hair – substances harder to dissolve into light than flesh and bones.

My mother's body, however, was still very much present, and on the third day we gave her a sky burial, the special funeral of Tibet where the body is offered to the vultures to eat. I wanted so much to go, to say my last farewell, but my father said I was too young. To my mind, that was absurd, he hadn't thought I was too young to be sent to Lhasa. But as always I had no choice.

Instead the task fell to the male members of my family. I watched while my oldest brother lifted my mother's body on to his back and started walking through lightly falling snow towards the famous Samye monastery. My brother and the small cortège were heading for Shitak Mountain, one of the holy peaks that rise above Samye. It's a very special, sacred mountain, reverberating with spiritual power, where hermits still manage to hide away in caves to meditate. My brother walked for seven hours with my mother on his back. He said he looked on the task as a way of purifying the negative karma he had accrued during his life – and as most of the way was uphill, he was probably right.

As my brother later described to me, they walked and walked in a solemn, reverential file. When they came to the beautiful Chongye River, they put my mother in a boat and rowed her across. Eventually Shitak Mountain came into sight and they began to climb to the *durto*, the charnel ground where sky burials take place. It was an even stretch of land high up on a ledge of the mountain, and upon it, at a distance from one another, were a number of flat boulders. These were the 'altars' where the bodies were placed ready for the ritual dissection. Sitting on various high outcrops of rock, keeping their distance, were the vultures.

My mother was handed over to the *ragyapas*, the clan who have performed sky burials for thousands of years, passing their art down the generations from father to son. Even among Tibetans they are regarded as a people apart, almost like outcasts – but they accept their place because they know they are performing a sacred duty. It is part of their job to take on the deceased person's suffering, so that others may live in peace. They do this every day of the week. I do not know how they can bear it.

The *ragyapas* put my mother, face down, on one of the flat stones and systematically, with great precision, began dismembering her. With scientific accuracy they cut her body into segments, first the limbs, then the torso. They flayed her skin, cut up her flesh and organs. Then they pulverised her bones, mixing them with the blood and flesh. To this they added barley flour to bind it all together. Last to be dismembered was her head. I was told that everything was carried out with great reverence and skill.

When they had done they began calling to the birds – a piercing, plaintive cry, my brothers said. That was the signal the vultures had been patiently waiting for. The *ragyapas* and the vultures had been working in harmony for so long they understood each other perfectly. As one, the birds launched themselves off their rocks, circled gracefully overhead and came gliding into the sky burial ground. They ate. My brothers reported that nothing of our mother remained, not even blood – only her clothes. The vultures had cleaned up every last bit of her.

Apparently other sky burials were being carried out at the same time and my brother noticed that the *ragyapas* offered the male bodies to the birds first. They told him male flesh is sourer than female flesh and if the vultures were given sweet female flesh first they would not touch the male corpses. For us, giving my mother a sky burial was not at all ghoulish, but was the best funeral we could give her. Some people bury their dead in the ground, where worms and maggots eat them. What is the difference? One you see, the other you don't. That's all. It is all a matter of belief.

To us sky burials are a special, sacred rite which no tourist is ever allowed to see. We believe that if you have a sky burial there is a good chance that you will be reborn as a human being, which is considered an excellent rebirth because you can achieve so much spiritually with it. So we felt we had done a wonderful thing for Mother. It was also a privilege and an achievement for our family. Not everyone can afford sky burials. You have to pay the *ragyapas* quite a lot of money, and my brother had saved up for a long time to be able to do this. In Tibet the second-best funeral is chopping up the body and throwing it in the water for the fish to eat – which is an act of generosity, but as a consequence Tibetans don't like eating fish. And the third-best is a cremation.

After my mother died a light went out in my life. Nothing was the same. I returned to Lhasa a different person. There was now nothing pulling me towards Yarlung, no nostalgia, no profound homesickness. The wonderful family home where I'd spent my early childhood had turned to dust. The new house was cold and empty, and no matter how many fires were lit I never felt warm there. My father was as remote as ever. My grandmother mourned so much that she died six months after my mother. My grandfather couldn't go on without his wife, and died three months after my grandmother. Now all my loved ones were dead. My world was bleaker than ever.

Yet, somewhere in the transition of my mother's death, I found my voice. I began to speak up to the Tashis. 'You treated me like an adult when I was only a kid. You are getting my labour for free,' I told them. 'You are getting a big mouth,' they retorted. I did not care any more. A new recklessness had entered into me. I had nothing to lose, and nothing really to live for.

In the meantime political unrest was brewing, and the atmosphere in Lhasa became extremely tense. More Westerners were arriving, bringing with them pictures of the Dalai Lama and the Panchen Lama as well as tapes of the Dalai Lama's teachings in India. These items stirred people up considerably. The pictures were pounced on as though they were gifts of precious jewels: some were tucked away in the folds of clothes, others found their way to the empty thrones of these revered figures and were draped in robes as if the lamas themselves were present. The devout would then make offerings of money and perform prostrations in front of the images. Even though those photographs were all that they had, the people's love and devotion to the Dalai Lama had not diminished in the least, despite the long years of oppression and persecution. Nor had our deepest need for the expression of our faith.

One morning in September 1987 I went to the market to buy vegetables and found myself caught up in a great commotion. A crowd of monks in their maroon and gold robes were marching down the street waving banners and shouting 'Long live the Dalai Lama.' I had never seen anything like it and had no idea what was going on. No one ever talked about politics in the Lhasa house, or indeed anywhere else in Tibet, and anyway I was at an age when politics did not interest me. There was no freedom of speech, nor any information on the radio or TV that would enable me to find out what was really happening.

Suddenly the police appeared and began to make some kind of fire by the side of the road. As the smoke curled up, I swallowed some of it and began to choke. Tears streamed down my face and I couldn't breathe. I thought I had been poisoned. It was tear gas, excruciatingly painful. 'Quick, run and put water on your face and get out of here!' a stall keeper yelled at me. The monks were arrested, of course, but afterwards everyone began talking about their courage, and became very excited.

The next month there was a much bigger demonstration. This time thousands of people took to the streets in protest about what was happening in Tibet under Chinese rule. It was as though the country had suddenly snapped and could not take it any more. I was nowhere near it, thank heavens, but I heard all about it. Some monks were arrested and taken to the central police station, which was then stormed and set on fire by a mob.

The repression that followed was brutal. Monks were shot or viciously beaten up in public. Many more were carted away to gulags, tortured and never seen again. It became known as the October Uprising, the biggest revolt since the invasion. The authorities were badly shaken and became more autocratic than ever. From now on when I went shopping I could see many more soldiers armed with weapons patrolling the streets and stationed on rooftops. And guns were permanently pointed down at us all from the roof of the Jokhang.

At the same time, young Tibetan monks whose parents had escaped in 1959 with the Dalai Lama and founded replica monasteries in India and Nepal, were also coming back to their homeland for short periods to see for themselves the land where their religion and their blood had originated. Their clean fresh robes, strong bodies, enthusiasm and vitality made a sad contrast to the poor, bedraggled, often demoralised monks who had never left. One fateful day I struck up a conversation with one such monk from Dharamsala, the Indian town where the Dalai Lama now lived and where he had set up his government-in-exile. He talked about it in glowing terms: 'In India you can pluck the most delicious fruit right off the trees. The Dalai Lama has done the most fantastic job for his people in India. There you can get an education for free, at the schools that he and his sister have established.'

What he said went home. Long after he left, his words kept

coming back to me. I began to think about escaping from Tibet. About finding the Dalai Lama. About freedom. About getting the education that I had been promised and which had been denied me for so long. To me education was the key to everything I lacked – my passport to a better life. Anything, I thought, had to be an improvement on what I had now.

When I looked ahead my future in Tibet looked bleak. Under Communism your entire life – your ability to earn a living, to buy food, to have somewhere to live – was dictated by your legal status. By moving from Yarlung to Lhasa when I was so young, I had lost out on all fronts. The Tashis had never got me City ID papers as they had promised (which would permit me food and living allowances in Lhasa) and I had lost my Country ID when I moved away from Yarlung. I belonged nowhere, I was officially a non-person with no rights whatsoever. This put me in a very precarious position. Even if I married I would never be free to live my own life; as custom decreed I would be obliged to serve the Tashis whenever they needed me. If I returned to Yarlung I had no lands allotted to me to till, and besides I had lost all my farming skills. Since the death of my mother and grandparents there was nothing holding me in Tibet any more.

I had absolutely no idea where India was. In my mind it was just another region of Tibet, only a bit further away. I was completely ignorant. But still, like Shangri-la, India beckoned.

CHAPTER SIX

Farewell Tibet

ONE DUSTY DAY in October 1988 my life changed. The day started off ordinarily enough with the usual long list of grinding, boring chores to do, but in the afternoon I was ordered to go to Sera monastery to offer butter lamps to the Buddhas. I was delighted. For once I would be blissfully on my own and have a few hours of freedom. I remember that day so clearly. I hopped on the bicycle, carrying the hot, liquid butter in a huge flask on my back. My job was to pour a few drops into as many of the burning butter lamps as I could. Deep down the Tashis were still religious, but because they worked for the police they didn't dare show it, and got me to make offerings on their behalf instead. As there are hundreds of butter lamps in Sera this ritual took me quite a long time.

I was absorbed in my task, and rather enjoying it, when I was distracted by the sound of whispering coming from a dark recess in one of the chapels. Curious, I crept closer to listen. Two youngish monks were huddled together in the semi-darkness, and as I eavesdropped I overheard them talking about a lorry they were going to use to escape from Tibet.

My heart leapt. Was this a chance for me to escape from my own miserable life too? Without thinking I grabbed that chance.

Showing myself, I blurted out, 'Please, take me with you.' The monks jumped, and stared at me in horror. The secret that they had guarded so carefully was out. 'What are you talking about?' they replied harshly, pretending nothing was afoot, making as if I was obviously deranged. 'Don't worry! Your secret is safe with me. I won't tell a soul,' I said quickly, hoping to reassure them.

The monks exchanged worried glances and looked anxiously behind me to see if the secret police were lurking in the shadows, waiting to pounce. I could so easily have been a spy sent to trap them. I hurriedly went on to tell them a little of my story – how I was used as a slave within a policeman's family, working all hours with no freedom, no wages and no prospects, and that I was willing to risk all, even my life, for a better future.

I talked fast, explaining the hopelessness of my situation – how I didn't have a work permit for either the city or the country and therefore had no chance of ever earning a living. I told them that my mother had recently died, how my family had given her a sky burial, and so there was no one to keep me in Tibet any more. They listened, and maybe something about the urgency of my voice and the sincerity of my heart softened their stern, anxious faces a little.

I talked on, telling them a little more about myself and my dreams. They hesitated and looked at each other, and they must have decided they could trust me. In quiet voices they admitted they had been planning their escape for months. 'Everything is arranged. We've organised for a lorry to take us to the border and then we're going over the Himalayas to Nepal and India,' they said. And they added the magic words, 'You may come with us.'

They went on to say I needed warm clothes and money to pay for the guide who would lead us over the mountains. Petrified that my only opportunity to escape was about to slip through my fingers, I said, 'No, no, I can come now, just as I am.' They smiled and reassured me that they were not leaving immediately and I really did need to take clothes and cash. I was to meet them, they said, at the Jokhang, at 3 am in two days' time.

The only photo that exists of my childhood in Tibet. My brother and I are in Norbu Linka, the summer residence of the Dalai Lama, during Saka Dawa, the high point of the Buddhist calendar.

With Ngawang Panchen, the torch-bearing monk who helped me escape through the mountains to Nepal and India.

My daughter Deckyi, aged 2½. Shortly afterwards I had
to give her away.

Two colleagues and me (left) in the Hotel Nataras in Dharamsala, where I found work.

With my landlord, who generously financed my journey to the Kalachakra to celebrate the birthday of the Dalai Lama.

In New Delhi with Shiri (left), the owner of the sari shop in which I worked.

I went home in a daze. I'd acted spontaneously, boldly, as was my nature – but now the reality of what I was about to do hit me. I was launching myself into the void. I was leaving my homeland and everything that was familiar and going I knew not where. I was young and very naïve. I had been locked up in the Tashis' family for nearly ten years. I was uneducated and had no idea what or where Nepal and India were. I knew of no one outside of Tibet except for a great-uncle in Kathmandu (my grandmother had told me his name and shown me a photograph of him). I had no identity papers and no travel permit, which was truly dangerous if I were stopped.

For the next two days my imagination went into overdrive. Informers were everywhere – especially in the monasteries, the hotbed of dissent against Chinese rule – and I began to think the police had somehow learnt of the monks' plans. In that case we would all have been arrested. I was terrified. Still, freedom beckoned stronger than fear. And so, over the next 48 hours, I went about my daily business as though nothing were afoot. Surreptitiously I took out the embroidered goatskin bag with tassels of yak hair dyed like a rainbow which my father had given to me when I left home, and put into it some warm clothing. I also took my mother's ring, which I had been given after her death, and sewed it into the waistband of my trousers. Wangmo, my girlfriend next door, was the only person I told, and she gave me a little money and bought me a pair of socks and cheap Chinese trainers from the market. She gave me so much strength and encouragement. If it had not been for her I would not have been able to do it.

On my last night in Lhasa I went to bed not thinking I would be able to sleep. But I did, and just before I woke I had an amazing dream. It was one of those rare dreams that doesn't fade with the morning light but stays with you for a long time, its image burned into your psyche. In my dream I was in a temple praying. I looked up and there in front of me was an enormous, golden Buddha about 200 feet high, sitting on a lotus flower. Reverently, I touched his feet and then raised my eyes. At that

moment the Buddha became real. He looked down at me, with
an indescribably loving expression on his face, and smiled. Then
I woke up, and my whole being was full of awe. The Buddha has
given me his blessing, I thought, maybe this is a sign that my
journey is going to be successful. It was 2.30 in the morning. In
spite of the dream I cried a little, because even I was nervous
about what I was about to do.

In Tibet when someone is leaving we have a custom of
putting a *katag*, the white scarf, around their neck to wish them
well on their journey, and pouring them a cup of tea. Since
there was no one to say goodbye to me, I put a *katag* around
my own neck, and poured a small cup of tea for myself. I
opened the door slowly and put the key back on the table. No
one stirred. Then I shut the door on my life and ran all the way
in the dark through the winding alleys to the Jokhang, 20
minutes away.

To my great relief the monks were there, waiting. Together we
made our way through the gloom of the ancient, holy temple
with its high ceilings and beautifully carved and painted woodwork. The air was thick and murky with incense smoke and the
smell of butter permeated everything, from centuries of burning butter lamps. We headed for the most revered statue in the
whole of Tibet, the exquisite, bejewelled Jowo Buddha, which
we Tibetans believe is a true representation of the Buddha himself. Before the Jowo we made three prostrations, praying that we
would be safe and would one day return to a happier Tibet.

Then we were ready to go. The lorry driver was parked
around the corner in a side street off the Barkhor. A thin,
middle-aged man with curly hair, he was carrying a load of
kerosene to the border town of Nyelam, more than 500 miles
away. Quickly he hid us in the back among the big metal drums
and covered us with a filthy, black, oily tarpaulin. We left the
capital behind and set off for our first stop.

Shigatse, 354 kilometres west of Lhasa, is reached only by
climbing the highest passes in Tibet. The scenery outside may
have been spectacular, but we never saw it. The journey was a

nightmare. For hours we bumped along the corrugated road, the so-called 'Freedom Highway', built by the Chinese but not tar-macked, and I hit my head against the drums at every jolt. Every bone of my body hurt. Dust came up through the floorboards, getting into our noses and eyes, caking us in a film of white powder so we looked like ghosts. To make things worse, we were inhaling the fumes from the kerosene and the lorry's exhaust. I felt very sick, but we didn't dare stick our heads out of the tar-paulin to get a breath of fresh air in case we were seen.

I began to get to know the monks. They were both about 30 or 35 and had been hiding in the countryside, having been involved in demonstrations against the Chinese. The reprisals had been brutal and monks were the number one target. Hun-dreds of them had been imprisoned, beaten, tortured and killed. These two were known to the police and were now fugitives. It had been out of sheer compassion that they had decided to take me with them. If we had been caught, 'abducting a young female' would have been added to the list of their crimes.

I never knew their names, I just called them *kushu*, which means 'monk', and in return they called me *poma*, or 'girl'. I can see their faces still. One was quite solid, and intelligent. He seemed the leader. The other was thinner and looked a little bit simple. I remember they both made lots of jokes to try and lighten things up.

Eventually the lorry pulled over and came to a halt. We had arrived in Shigatse, the driver's regular stopping point, where he planned to spend the night. After much whispered discussion about what we should do, the monks eventually decided to risk getting out. Shigatse was the second biggest town in Tibet and they thought we could easily lose ourselves among the crowds. Besides, they needed to buy provisions for the journey – and we all desperately needed to stretch our legs and get some fresh air after that horrible cramped ride. The monks went off on their own, telling me not to wander far and to meet them back at the lorry by dusk, when the driver said he would take us to a safe guesthouse for the night.

I looked about, eager to see what Shigatse was like. I didn't much like what I found. There was an ominous, menacing feeling hanging in the air. Shigatse was a politically important place, since for centuries it had been the traditional home of the Panchen Lamas. The Panchen Lamas were extremely powerful figures, second only in importance to the Dalai Lama and much revered and loved. The last one, the Tenth Panchen Lama, had been a controversial figure. At the beginning of the occupation he had stated that he had faith in the good intentions of the Chinese leadership. But then he had been captured, publicly humiliated, paraded through the streets and spat on. After that he disappeared to China where he tried to work with the government, but was imprisoned again, in solitary confinement. On his release he had married a Chinese woman. This caused a big scandal in Tibet. We Tibetans were never sure of his allegiances (until a little later when he returned to Tibet and spoke up for his people. But that was after I had left).

I don't know whether it was because of the last Panchen Lama's fiery diatribe about the devastating effect of Chinese rule in Tibet, or because of his close links to Beijing, but Shigatse had been turned into a garrison town, more so even than Lhasa. Soldiers and police, both Chinese and Tibetan, strutted about everywhere with guns, and military music blared from every street corner. Still, I was a silly young girl who had no clue about the workings of the world, and I decided I would go off to the fabulous Tashi Lhunpo monastery to see the giant statue of the future Buddha, the Maitreya. Twenty-six metres high, it was famous throughout all Tibet.

I was on my way there, gawping with my mouth open at what I saw, standing out like a tourist, when I was stopped by a soldier. 'What are you doing?' he barked. 'Where do you live? You don't belong here. If you are escaping, you are a criminal and I am taking you to jail.'

I froze. If I opened my mouth my accent would be a dead giveaway. He would instantly know that I came from Lhasa and should not be in Shigatse without documentation. At that moment a big Khampa from east Tibet walked by. The Khampas are a swashbuckling, fearless warrior tribe who waged a fierce guerrilla war against the invaders, and he was wearing the traditional red strings in his long black hair, a sword at his side, and his jacket thrown casually over one arm. 'Don't worry, she is my sister, she is with me,' he said, taking my arm firmly and steering me quickly away.

When I thanked him he patted my shoulder and said, 'You're OK, don't worry. I know exactly where you are heading – I take people out.' It was an incredible near miss, and it made me realise how stupid I had been to make myself so obvious. The big Buddha from my dream must be looking after me.

Subdued and shaken, I returned to the lorry and waited for the two monks. One returned, the other, the leader, didn't. They had split up after they left me – I never found out why. We stayed waiting for an extra day, but he never came back. He had obviously been captured. I didn't like to think about what was happening to him, and I felt incredible sadness for this man who had risked his own safety to help me. But the driver had to be on his way and so we had no choice but to get back into the lorry and continue.

Now there were only two of us, both overwhelmed by anxiety. I was really scared. Had the monk talked under torture, revealed there were others escaping with him? The soldier's words echoed around my head: 'You are a criminal, you will go to jail.' I thought of my bed back in Lhasa. It was only a mattress on the kitchen floor but at least it was somewhere safe. I thought of Wangmo next door. I might have made a big mistake. But there was no turning back.

After Shigatse the road became even steeper, crossing the high passes to reach the Tibetan plateau. We were thrown about in the back as the lorry ground its gears, painfully climbing to over 17,000 feet. Suddenly it stopped. The driver peered under the tarpaulin. 'Quick, get out! Have a look and say a prayer!'

The sight was breathtaking. Laid out before us in a continuous line stretching east to west across the horizon were the jagged, snow-covered peaks of the high Himalaya, our planet's highest peaks. The roof of the world. This was my home, my special home, and I was leaving it. The sun shone in a sky so blue it was indigo, and the air was crystalline, sparkling, like champagne. We breathed it in, in huge thankful gulps. Brightly coloured prayer flags fluttered in the wind, sending out prayers to all corners of the universe. 'May the gods be victorious!' we cried, the traditional prayer of all Tibetan travellers crossing the high passes.

Then it was back under the airless, filthy tarpaulin and on with our sickening ride. At this altitude we could now add piercing cold to our physical and mental discomfort. At night the temperature dropped below freezing and I would sit in the back, shivering madly, my hands and feet numb with the bitter, piercing cold. I had only brought a light padded Chinese jacket and a thin black coat, and they were woefully inadequate. To combat these temperatures I needed a thick, down coat, woollen gloves and hat. For the first time I began to sense that I was gambling with my life.

Whenever he could, the driver would stop and bring us into the front cabin with him to thaw out. He was wonderful. He didn't charge us anything for the ride, and often bought us food at truck stops along the way. He would say to me, 'I can understand the monks wanting to escape, but why you? You're young. You're not in trouble. I've been to Nepal and the food isn't so good and the place smells funny too. But if this is what you wish, then it's my duty to help you.' And on he drove.

From now until the border the road became truly dangerous. It was dotted with checkpoints, and the men manning them were those we most feared, the *burtsun chenpos*, a people's militia set up to seek out spies, counter-revolutionaries and those trying to escape to India. This was the main route to Nepal and the most obvious escape route both for wanted Tibetans, and those, like myself, who merely sought freedom and a better life. The driver would stop well before each checkpoint and let us out, we would walk a long way around and meet up with him on the other side. He would wait by the side of the road pretending his lorry had broken down.

The detours sometimes took us two or three hours at time, and while we were struggling across the terrain the remaining monk and I became closer. We would walk together up the mountains and through the streams. He carried my shoes when we had to wade through water, holding my hand when the going got tough. By this stage I was not only cold and wet but drained as well. It wasn't so much the climbing, more the accumulated tension and fear for our missing companion.

Finally we reached Nyelam, the last town in Tibet. It's a bustling border town clinging to the hillside about 10,000 feet above sea level, full of traders, porters and travellers. It sits above the Friendship Bridge, which divides Tibet from Nepal. Freedom was only a few steps away, but that bridge was teeming with police and soldiers – and for us it was totally impassable. The monk and I discussed our best course of action with the driver. 'The only way for you to get into Nepal is to bypass the bridge completely by taking a back route over the mountains,' he said.

It was the end of our journey with our driver, but before he left us he did us one more supreme kindness – he introduced us to woman who ran a guesthouse and who took in escapees. He said she could be trusted. 'It's extremely dangerous for just the two of you to go, there's safety only in numbers. There are many robbers and villains in the mountains waiting for escaping Tibetans. You're easy prey. They will take all your possessions, rape the girl and leave you stranded. You must wait for others to join you. This landlady will organise an experienced guide who knows the way and who can be trusted not to tip off the bandits.'

So we settled down to find others who could join us. Our landlady was a fat, jolly woman with a strong face and big, rough working hands. Her guests were mainly lorry drivers, and we all slept together in one room on the floor, like a family. I used my bag as a pillow; there was not much in it but I didn't want to lose the little I had. It was a hectic household with lots of comings and goings.

After we had been there about a week my companion, who was really not very bright, and had about as much clue as me as to how the world worked, went out one morning to buy provisions for our journey, as he'd heard another group of escapees was about to arrive. He never came back. What could I think except that he too had been caught? I was devastated. Both monks who had taken me out of Lhasa, and who had looked after me, were now facing the most appalling fate.

I didn't like to think about what they were going through – the beatings, the electric cattle prods, the arms tied tightly behind the back and then yanked up until the shoulders broke (a favourite torture of the Chinese in Tibet). Over the last few days the second monk and I had become especially close, like a brother and sister. We had been through so much together. Now I was the only survivor of our small group – I didn't know why. The brutal truth was that I was totally on my own, with no idea what to do or where to turn.

Feeling vulnerable beyond measure, I was terrified to leave the house. I imagined that the Tashi family had telephoned every station from Lhasa to the border, circulating my description, and that the moment I stepped out of the door I'd be recognised and arrested. Nepal and India seemed further away than ever – an impossible fantasy. As I had learnt at the Tashis', however, I kept my fear locked up inside of me. I made sure I was cautious and very respectful to the landlady, for my fate rested in her hands. I helped her with the chores, engaged her in conversation and gradually gained information from her about the escape routes.

Two weeks later no other escapees had turned up and the landlady informed me I had better go back to Lhasa. I'd rather kill myself, I thought. There was nothing to go back to. I had no choice but to go on. In desperation, a plan began to take shape in my mind. I recalled that one day, while helping my landlady do the washing at the river, she had pointed to a mountain and said that that was the secret way out of Tibet to Nepal. I looked at it and it didn't seem so high to me. I've climbed higher mountains than that, I thought. I decided to take the risk and go it alone.

A few nights later, having said nothing to anyone, I left her house, leaving my bag and everything behind so as not to arouse suspicion. I carried nothing except the clothes I stood up in and two packets of biscuits. I arrived at the river around 7.30 pm and hid in the bushes, waiting for it to get dark. The crickets were loud, but I stayed as quiet as a mouse. At 8.30 pm the moon started to rise. I braced myself. *I will go on my own across the mountain. I will go now!*

As I began to move, a torch suddenly shone on my face and a voice said, 'Are you escaping?' I froze. It was a man wearing a woolly hat and gloves, the outfit typically worn by undercover policemen. Petrified, I had to make a fast decision – to tell the truth or not. Something inside urged me to own up. 'Yes,' I replied.

'Where is your group then?' the figure demanded. I told him my companion had been taken away a few days ago, and that I was leaving by myself. The torch bearer hesitated and then said to me: 'It's true. I saw a man being jumped on by Chinese guards the other day. I watched as they beat him around the head with sticks and kicked him in the back. Then they took him away.' I knew then that this was not a secret policeman. Tentatively, I asked if he were escaping too. 'Yes,' he replied, 'my group is higher up the mountain. They went into hiding when we heard your footsteps.' 'May I come with you?' I asked tentatively. 'Of course,' the torch bearer replied.

It seemed that karma had once again provided me with escape companions. There were seven in all – one other woman aged about 28, and six men aged between 25 and 40. I was clearly the baby of the bunch. We didn't ask many questions of each other. It was better not to know much, and besides, that is not the way with Tibetans, especially when we're travelling. We do not get involved in someone's personal history.

I did learn, however, that some of the men were fugitive monks, although none was wearing robes. The torch bearer's name was Ngawang Panchen, and he came from the Nechung monastery in Lhasa. He'd also been caught up in a demonstration and was fleeing for his life. The woman was going to marry a lama who had left Tibet for Kathmandu and de-robed. They'd hired a Sherpa, who knew the secret paths out of Tibet and whose price was 3,000 Nepali rupees from each of them – a huge amount of money. I gave what money I had; it was not enough, but the others helped me with the rest. Truly, I met such unbelievable kindness. My heart was full of gratitude.

CHAPTER SEVEN

Escape

W E STARTED TO CLIMB by moonlight. Up and up the mountain side we went, Ngawang Panchen and another man using torches to light the way. I soon discovered that for me it was easier to see by the moon, as the torch only lit up a small patch of ground and I was always tripping over stones and roots. It was a silent, silvery world, with the moon shining on bushes and leaves, making everything ethereal and mystical. We kept walking through the night, not speaking much, but moving very fast in order to get as far away as possible from the police in Nyelam. I had no idea where I was going, only that it was steeply up.

With the rising of the sun I found myself in an entirely new world. It was beautiful. I was in deep jungle. All my life I had lived surrounded by countryside that was like a lunar landscape – bare, brown, dry and dusty, with hardly a tree or a blade of grass in sight. But this mountain bordering Nepal was at a lower altitude and was covered with lush, thick trees and bushes. Everything was green. It was magic. I looked around me in wonderment. The trees were tall and dense, their branches interlocking overhead so that they made a complete canopy. I peered above me trying to see the sun, but it was completely blotted out. Here in the jungle I had entered a gloomy, semi-dark realm with mists swirling around from the low clouds that shrouded the mountain. The whole atmosphere was moist and foggy.

As we walked, large drops of water dripped down on us from the thick foliage, making our clothes and our faces wet. Underfoot the leaves and vines had rotted to make a thick, moist carpet. It felt springy and strange, like walking on a sofa. The smell was weird too, pungent with the aroma of decaying vegetation. The din of the crickets was overwhelming. It was an entirely different quality of sound. In Tibet, the air is vast and spacious, so that sound moves around freely. In this forest, however, closed in by the density of the trees, it sounded as though I had been put into a big earthenware pot with the stopper in.

As I peered into the half-light I noticed groves of huge bamboo, as big as a man's waist. Children at school used to write with bamboo pens. Now I knew where they came from. And I looked in astonishment at the vast quantities of dead wood just lying around. In Tibet wood is a very precious commodity. I cast my mind back to the children of my village who would set off for days looking for wood for their stoves. If only they could see this, I thought.

I set off at a cracking pace, my spirits high, my mind full of wonder at the jungle and my extraordinary fortune at getting this far against seemingly insuperable odds. For the first time I smelt freedom. Thoughts of the education and the life I could have in India raced around my head. I was young, I was strong, I was full of hope.

We kept walking through that first day as well, too frightened to stop until we had put a good distance between us and Nyelam. There was no path to speak of but every footstep was a new discovery. We had to push our way through the dripping undergrowth, following our guide. Once we had reached the peak of the mountain we slid and slithered our way down the other side. Going down was actually more difficult than climbing up, and I frequently fell flat on my bottom, which was quite embarrassing. Still, it was like a game, tumbling down the mountain as if

I was a little girl. At the bottom we found a small stream which we had to cross. Luckily it was quite shallow and there were large stones to step on. Halfway over we stopped to drink the clear cold water. It tasted bitter, due I think to all the leaves and roots that fallen into it.

Once safely across I looked up and saw in front of me another huge mountain soaring into the sky. That was when I realised my big mistake. In that moment the startling truth hit me that freedom didn't lie on the other side of the mountain that the landlady had shown me, as I had naïvely imagined when I set out. I had thought that if I climbed that then I would be free. I really knew nothing!

I asked where we going and was told that our route to freedom lay in turning west and traversing the high ranges of Nepal, skirting all roads and towns, until we came out near Kathmandu. I did not know it then, but it was going to be an exceedingly long journey. And it dawned on me, like a kick in the stomach, that I certainly would have died if I had set off on my own as I intended. There was no way that a single person, let alone an uneducated, ignorant girl, with no provisions and no knowledge of geography, could have survived that trek.

I took a deep breath at the sight of this massive mountain towering above me and set off up the almost perpendicular slope. My energy was still high. Every Tibetan has a natural aptitude for climbing. It is born in us, and our blood is supercharged with haemoglobin from having to acclimatise to scarce oxygen, so that mountaineering is relatively easy for us. Still, in that terrain our progress was slow. The jungle was as thick as ever, and the light as gloomy. The mist continued to swirl about us, making the way difficult to see. Sometimes the vines and bushes became so impenetrable that the guide had to hack his way through with a machete. It was hard work for him, but easier for us without the bushes clawing at us. We might not have known where we were, but our guide seemed to know exactly where he was going.

Night fell for the second time. Once again we did not stop,

but kept walking by the light of the torches and the moon, through the moist dripping trees and thick bushes. I was becoming tired by now but adrenalin and excitement spurred me on. Dawn brought more mountain, more jungle, more mist, more wetness, more vines, more thorn bushes. We walked and walked, up and down, crossing another stream whose water we drank again.

And then, thankfully, in a small clearing of the jungle we stopped. The guide deemed it was now safe for us to take a break. My companions began opening their biscuits and *tsampa* – which they could only mix with water, not tea as was customary – and shared what they had with me. I wasn't very hungry, and took little – my stomach was too full of tension. Besides, I was embarrassed to take much because I had only two packets of biscuits to offer in return.

Finally we were allowed to sleep. Of course none of us had sleeping bags or camping equipment, and the ground was far too wet to lie down on. The others, who were carrying their few belongings in bags, sat down on them and tried to rest, but I, who had brought nothing, could only squat down on my haunches, close my eyes and sleep like a chicken. It was not very restful!

In fact none of us got any real sleep during the whole time we were travelling. But this was the pattern that we would follow from now on – walking during the night and resting during the day. Although it was unbelievably difficult cutting through that jungle in the dark and climbing up and down perilously steep slopes, it was what we had to do. It was simply too dangerous for us to be out and about in daylight. We may not have seen anyone in that dense jungle, but we often heard voices in the distance and knew that habitation was not far away. It added considerably to our tension.

After a few hours we were on our way again. It was still daylight when came across a grove full of monkeys. They were fantastic, large and grey with beautiful white faces and long beards. Their coats were shiny and their eyes bright. They sat in the branches of the trees silently watching us. I'd never seen anything like them before and I stood entranced in their midst. We stayed there for quite a long time, watching them back. They made a welcome break from the relentless climbing and quite refreshed my spirits.

One other fortunate aspect of our escape was the weather. In Tibet, November is cold and dry but here in the jungle it was wet and warm, so that my thin padded jacket was more than adequate. I realised that the monks whom I had originally set out with knew exactly what they were doing when they chose this time of the year to escape. Any earlier and we would have caught the monsoon, whose deluges cause frequent mudslides that kill many travellers crossing the mountains. Any later and we would have been trapped by the snows and risked freezing to death.

As the days wore on my euphoria wore off. The jungle seemed endless as we trudged and hacked our way through it for mile after tedious mile. We were all getting increasingly tired and I began bitterly to regret that I had walked so quickly in the first days. The tall trees continued to make everything dark, murky, sodden and dank. Their branches were frequently entangled, while thorns ripped at our clothes and arms as we passed. We learnt to use the trailing branches and the curly tap roots as ropes to haul us up. We would let go of one and make a grab for the next one higher up. Sometimes they came away in my hand and I'd go tumbling down the slope until a bush or tree stopped me. Then I had to start clambering up all over again.

Coming down became more treacherous the more tired we became. The ground was muddy and slippery and we found it wasn't much use trying to grab vines or roots. It was easier simply to roll or slide down as best we could. Now it no longer felt like a game. Our clothes and bodies were filthy, and our shoes became caked with mud. We were perpetually soaked through from the constant fog and the moisture that dripped on us from the foliage. We became increasingly uncomfortable, and our spirits were low. How I wished there was a cave for us to creep into to get out of our drenched surroundings and have a long, dry sleep. Unfortunately on this route out, there were no caves available. And at the bottom of each mountain there was yet another small stream, making our feet even wetter. I tried to think positively – at least we didn't have to negotiate lurching, broken-down old rope bridges suspended above raging torrents, or walk along slippery tree trunks placed over rivers, like those that exist in many parts of Tibet. And then we started the long gruelling ascent yet again through dense, tangled jungle.

We may have been a band of strangers but we got on well together. There were no fights, no arguments, no problems, in spite of the tension of our situation. Why should there be? Tibetans are not accustomed to thinking 'I don't like him, I can't stand her.' We don't get caught up in that sort of psychology, our minds are flexible, open. There are no words in Tibetan for 'needing attention'; we have bad people and seriously mad people, but there are no such things as neuroses in Tibet. I think one reason is because we don't have time. The effort simply to stay alive keeps us physically occupied from dawn to dusk, so that there is no time for the monkey mind to start playing up. Just to make a cup of tea takes two hours!

And so our escape was not like those Western reality TV shows where one person can't stand another's personality. Instead we resembled a band of pilgrims, united in our common cause of seeking freedom. We helped each other along, not talking much, but saying under our breath the mantra of compassion, the special mantra of Tibet, *om mani padme hum*, 'hail to the jewel in the lotus'. It bonded us and kept us going.

However, the optimism I had on the first few days of the escape quickly gave way to constant worry. Would I ever get out of these mountains and this jungle? What was going to happen to me? Was there really a Tibetan government somewhere in India? Did the Dalai Lama truly live there? Did my family know I had gone? Were they worried about me? We all felt similar anxieties, and these questions became the main topic of discussion whenever we stopped.

I felt as though I had died and entered the Bardo state, suspended between two worlds. In front of me was an unknown future, behind me a traumatic past. Even here in the jungle my past haunted me. If ever I managed to fall asleep squatting on my haunches I had a recurring nightmare of being back with the Tashis. In my dream they were always ordering me to do something or scolding me for something I had not done and I would wake up in a fright, ready to leap up and do what they told me. Then I would realise I was far away, in the dripping, musty, rotting jungle covered over by trees and shrouded in mist, wet and tired, and wonder if it were any better. You are really gambling with your life, I thought.

The physical danger was as real as the mental and emotional dangers. Although we may not have seen a single living person apart from each other since we had set off, that did not mean there were no human beings about. Often we would hear a shout in the distance, and know there were workmen, shepherds, villagers or even police patrols not far away. Then we were all terrified that we would be found. We stood still in our tracks and waited for a gang of men to appear. We knew, without doubt, that if we were spotted we would be robbed, raped, handed back to the Chinese – or all three. The locals who lived in these mountains were poor, and escaping Tibetans were a welcome source of extra income. The reward we would bring might boost their earnings a hundredfold. When no one came into view we continued walking, a little less confident, considerably more tense. The longer we were out there, the less I felt our good fortune would last.

It wasn't just humans who posed a threat. There was the constant danger of being killed by animals too. One day when we were resting I saw a long yellow and black snake slither down a tree and come towards me. I jumped up so fast! We don't have snakes in Tibet. It slipped straight past me into the undergrowth. The guide kindly told me it was poisonous. As though on cue, after that I seemed to see snakes everywhere. Now I have to worry about being eaten by wild animals, I thought.

In fact the jungle was home to several big wild cats – mountain lions, tigers and lynx. At night we could hear them grunting and growling in the bushes – we didn't know how far away they were. One day, as were climbing in single file, a tiger walked straight in front of us. It was so magnificent, strong and powerful that I forgot to be afraid. Later, when I realised what had happened, I began shivering with fright. After that I made sure I went in the middle of the group. I didn't want to be the last one in line, to be grabbed by a wild beast from behind.

To me the greatest nightmare of all, however, were the revolting ubiquitous leeches. The first time I encountered them was early on – in that soggy, damp jungle they reigned supreme. I looked down and saw a thin red worm swaying from my chin. It had attached itself by one end to my skin and was sucking up my blood, leaving the rest of its body going round and round in front of my eyes. There was another on my cheek, and another and another – all weaving about on my face. I screamed! It was dangerous to make such a noise but I couldn't help it. I felt I was being attacked by an alien life force. Your body is usually only eaten by creatures when you are dead, but these 'worms' were eating me alive.

The leeches got everywhere – into my trousers, my top and most of all my shoes. How they loved my juicy feet and toes, made doubly wet by walking on the rotting, soaked jungle floor and by my own perspiration from the relentless climbing. I'd look down and see my socks covered in blood. Those leeches were arguably the most traumatic thing of the entire escape. I discovered to my disgust that if I tried to pull them off, they would leave their heads behind in my skin. I had to wait for the guide, who smoked, to come and burn them off with his cigarettes. They were one living creature I never learnt to love, in spite of my Buddhist beliefs.

We pressed on, up and down those seemingly endless mountains, trusting that the guide knew where he was leading us. About two weeks into our escape he suddenly abandoned us in the middle of the jungle, saying he knew a shepherd who lived not far away in a hut on the mountain and he was going to bring us back some extra food. We waited for hours, convinced that either he had disappeared for good, leaving us at the mercy of the jungle, or that he was going to return with a band of thugs. We had endless discussions about how we could defend ourselves, but they were fruitless as we had no weapons and nowhere to run. Finally he did come back – bringing some rice and dhal wrapped up in leaves. It wasn't much but we devoured it with glee. I gave thanks that my group had picked an honest guide.

As the days and weeks wore on our provisions naturally grew increasingly meagre and I suppose we all began to starve. We were down to eating mostly biscuits by now. I was still not hungry and didn't mind the lack of food very much. But we were also extremely tired and weak from the relentless climbing, from being constantly wet through from the mist and the soaked foliage, from being torn by thorns, and from falling having lost our foothold on the sodden, slippery, muddy slopes. By this stage my fellow escapees decided to jettison their bags. They were getting too weak to carry them. I'd set off with nothing, so I didn't have that problem. But one day I lingered behind a little because I wanted to go to the toilet – I was still very shy about such matters. To my horror the others disappeared out of sight. They spent hours looking for me, calling my name, and were very upset when they found me.

We had been walking for about two weeks when my Chinese trainers began to fall apart under the strain. Soon they were completely useless. I showed them to Ngawang Panchen: 'Look at my shoes! They've disintegrated. What on earth am I going to do?' He instantly replied, 'Wear mine. I have another pair.' Such extraordinary kindness! However, they were far too big. My feet began to slide about inside them and soon started to really hurt. The wetness of my feet and shoes didn't help. When we climbed up my heels took a battering, going down it was my toes. Soon my feet were blistered and bleeding.

I was in a pretty bad state, and now we arrived at the highest mountain yet. It was not enveloped in jungle but bare above the tree line, its peak covered in snow. I looked up at its dizzying height and sincerely wondered if I could make it. I was weak with exhaustion and my feet and legs were in agony. I took a deep breath and forced myself to start the climb. Every step took all my strength and will power as I hauled myself up those vertical slopes. My legs ached with an unimaginable tiredness, my calves swelled to twice their normal size, my feet were bleeding and so sore that it was like walking on shards of glass. I was in such pain that my whole body was crying out in agony. It was a supreme pain, accompanied by a kind of mental panic. I never imagined I could suffer so much. I forced myself on – not daring to look at the top, just concentrating on taking one step at a time. Still, I never cried, nor complained.

Finally, I don't know how, I reached the top. There I found a beautiful lake and, spread out before me, the glorious breathtaking snow-capped high Himalaya. Among them was the most magnificent peak of all, known by Westerners as Everest but which we Tibetans call Chomolungma, 'Mother Goddess of the Earth'. I felt that surely I had been in the Bardo and had now arrived in the Pure Realm, the Buddhist heaven, where all suffering has ceased and perpetual peace and love reigns supreme. I was so high, on top of the world, like being in an aeroplane, and my mind was suddenly filled with a sensation of infinite space. An eagle was flying overhead and I watched as a deer came down to drink from the water's edge. I found a rock, sat down on it, and decided I was going no further. This was paradise. I'm staying here, I thought. I'm not going any further. I don't care any more about getting to India or having an education. Maybe I'll die of starvation or the wild animals will eat me, I don't mind. Just so long as I don't have to move.

I didn't care. I'd given up and was prepared to die. In this wonderful place death would be peaceful. I wasn't scared. I was just numb, utterly blank.

Ngawang Panchen turned round and saw me. 'Come on. Get up. Walk!' he ordered. 'Please go on, I can't take another step, my legs won't move,' I replied. 'Try one footstep,' he said. 'No. Really, I can't,' I replied. With that he came back, lifted me up and carried me down the mountain.

As we descended we left the bare terrain of the high mountain and entered the jungle again, and he set me down by a river. There, for the first and only time, we lit a fire to make tea. It wasn't real Tibetan tea, just black tea with a little bit of butter in it, but it tasted wonderful, and felt worth the risk of giving away our whereabouts. We ate the last of the *tsampa*, which gave me strength. We stayed by the river for two nights and three days until I had recovered sufficiently to continue. It was the longest time we ever stopped, and they did it for me.

Then we were on our way again, climbing more jungle-covered mountains for another week. I walked by sheer will power. I often felt like giving up but all the time Ngawang Panchen kept urging me on. 'If you walk over the next mountain the Dalai Lama is waiting for us. He has tea for us,' he would encourage me. I would get excited. But then there was no one, nothing – just another mountain. He would continue, 'Definitely over this mountain the Dalai Lama will welcome us.' That's how I kept going.

By now we were well into Nepal and small mountain villages were becoming more frequent, which brought new danger. At times we had to come out of hiding and pass right in front of houses. We went in twos and threes, walking very, very quickly. It was obvious by our looks and clothes that we were escaping Tibetans but we got away with it. There was so much to fear, but nothing was as bad as the relentless climbing.

One day we saw a road with traffic and knew we were close to Kathmandu. Our guide turned and announced, 'We are almost there.' When we came nearer he took four of the group on to a bus to deliver them to the Tibetan refugee camp, and instructed the rest of us to stay hidden and wait. He came back and reported that the first group had arrived safely. Now it was our turn. I imagined we stood out like sore thumbs as we got on the bus. For the first time since I had set off, my luck

changed. At one of the many checkpoints some Nepali police
got on. 'Passports, papers,' they said, clicking their fingers as they
walked down the aisle. Of course we didn't have papers, and we
couldn't speak one word of Nepali – not even 'thank you' or
'sorry'. A policeman looked at us and shouted 'China, China!'
We were caught.

They led us off the bus, took us to the police station and
asked us our names. We told them stupid things: 'chicken',
'horse', 'donkey'. They strip-searched us, looking for money and
valuables. Having been strictly brought up and being extremely
modest, I was deeply humiliated. They looked in the soles of our
shoes, in the seams of our clothes – everywhere. One guard
checked my long plaited hair, and then he touched my breast. I
was naked but furious. I swore at him. 'Do that again and I'll
kick you in the balls!' I cried. I don't know if he understood me,
but he got the message.

He found my mother's ring hidden in my waistband and took
it. Afterwards they locked us up and we spent the night wondering what was going to happen. They were either going to
imprison us for good or send us back to Tibet, or China as they
called it. At 6 am they took us out to a small red police car. We
set off, apparently heading back to the border, but they said,
'Kathmandu, no China.' Amazingly, they were telling the truth.
Having taken all our jewellery and the little money we had, in
return they were giving us a lift. I guess they felt it was a fair
exchange – it was probably a scam they carried out with many
escaping Tibetans. We were waved past the checkpoints and
dumped in the middle of Kathmandu. It was unbelievably noisy,
dirty and dusty; we didn't have a clue where we were.

In all the journey had taken seven weeks: one week to Nyelam, three weeks in Nyelam, and three weeks escaping over the
mountains. When I look back I am astonished at how brave I
was at that age. Generally I have a happy nature, which helped
in those days of escape. Being separated from my family, watching my mother die as a little girl, and living and working with
strangers who showed me no affection made me strong. All the

time I was climbing those never-ending mountains I prayed to the Buddha: 'Thank you for freeing my life, for showing me the paths to go.' I kept in my heart the image of the smiling Buddha who had appeared in my dream the night I left Lhasa. I believe that in 1988 my karma had ripened. Everything had come together for my escape. It was my destiny to leave. My mind was clear and so was the path.

But now, on that morning in Kathmandu, I had nothing except my clothes. And my freedom? I did not know it then, but I had many more mountains yet to climb.

CHAPTER EIGHT

First Taste of Freedom

WE SET OFF TOWARDS BOUDHANATH, a suburb of Kathmandu where we had heard there was a Tibetan refugee centre. I was totally exhausted from the escape, my feet were in agony, and I was numb from the ordeal in the police station, but even so, the sights and sounds of Kathmandu sent my senses reeling. I'd never experienced anything like it. I thought I had arrived on another planet. It was utter pandemonium. Rickety trucks painted in rainbow colours, modern motor cars, ancient buses, motorbikes and auto rickshaws wove madly in and out, blowing their horns and belching acrid black smoke. The noise and mayhem after the isolation of the jungle was incredible.

Dogs, cats, cows and children mingled with the vehicles, not seeming at all worried for their safety. And that mass of humanity! I did not know there were so many people in the world. There were thousands and thousands of them, sitting in tiny shops, doing business or simply milling about. Dust flew everywhere. It was worse than in Tibet. And there was a strange smell in the air too, which soon made me feel quite sick and gave me a pounding headache. I wondered what it could be, and then I noticed little plumes of smoke wafting from doorways and realised it was incense. We have masses of incense in Tibet, but this was sickly sweet, not like the aromatic wood and juniper we burn.

And then I saw the most astonishing sight of all – a totally naked man came into view, walked right down the road and past us. He was skeleton-thin, covered in ash from head to toe, his hair in long matted dreadlocks, and he did not seem at all embarrassed. I couldn't believe my eyes. One of my party told me he was a sadhu, an Indian holy man, an ascetic, who had renounced every material comfort of life, including his clothes. I wondered what I'd let myself in for.

We didn't know where we were going. The roads were all higgledy-piggledy and wove through houses packed together in an endless stream of habitation. We walked for miles saying 'Boudhanath, Boudhanath' and following people's pointed fingers. Eventually, towering over the rooftops and satellite dishes, we saw the Great Stupa of Boudhanath, a huge white dome with fabulous bright blue Buddha eyes painted on all sides as if surveying the entire Kathmandu valley. It was the biggest Buddhist stupa outside of Tibet – the landmark we'd been looking for. Our spirits soared and our pace quickened. More and more Tibetan prayer flags came into view and we knew we had arrived.

My relief at finally getting there was palpable. I could see at a glance that Boudhanath was a complete Tibetan colony, with shops selling Tibetan wares, Tibetans of all ages walking around the stupa, turning the prayer wheels at its base, fingering their prayer beads, doing prostrations. In stark contrast to the Tibet I had just left, they seemed free and uninhibited. But then there were no Chinese police and no cameras looking on.

At the refugee centre I found Ngawang Panchen, the monk with the torch, who had taken the first bus into Kathmandu. I almost burst into tears, I was so happy to see him. But this was no time to start letting my dammed-up emotions out. I was far from home, I didn't know where I was, I was tired beyond comprehension, I was sad and relieved at once, and I felt increasingly unwell. I did not know what it was but I was becoming fever-ish, cold one minute, sweating the next.

They took my photograph, registered my name and asked which part of Tibet I was from. 'Lhasa,' I replied. I didn't know what else to say. Where *did* I belong? They gave me some second-hand clothes and some food, which I could not eat. They also gave me enough money to get to Swayambhunath, a suburb of Kathmandu, where my great-uncle Ngawang Tomden lived. He had no idea that I even existed, let alone that I was coming, but he was family and on those grounds I trusted that he would take me in.

I found him in a small house at the foot of the great temple of Swayambhunath, a towering edifice perched on top of a hill and swarming with hundreds of monkeys. Like everything in Kathmandu the temple was extremely ancient – so old it looked as if it might crumble into dust at any moment. My great-uncle was utterly amazed – and delighted – to see me. Tall, handsome and still very young looking, he'd been a senior monk in Tibet until he had escaped with the Dalai Lama in the great exodus. He was now wearing lay person's clothes and, I discovered, was the tutor to one of Tibet's most eminent, high reincarnated lamas, Serkong Dorje Chang, who was about four years old and who lived with him.

I managed a little polite conversation, telling him the bare bones of my escape and news of the family. Then I fainted. My great-uncle picked me up and put me to bed, where I fell into a feverish, fitful sleep. I was literally half dead with exhaustion and the trauma of all that had happened in the past few weeks. Now I knew I was safe I could let go. I slept for 15 days, my uncle nursing me. Much of the time I was delirious, drifting in and out of consciousness, not knowing where I was. It was a strange half-world where everything was far away, seen though a veil of mist. My feet and legs were in a terrible state, swollen, red and raw from chafing, excruciatingly painful. I could not bear to wear shoes.

One day, when I thought I was better, I went up to the roof

only to faint again. Luckily a neighbour, who was pegging out washing on another roof nearby, saw me fall and came rushing over to tell my great-uncle. He tried to give me some butter tea, but I couldn't drink it; made with the Kathmandu water, it tasted awful. I couldn't eat anything either, because my stomach had shrunk from having nothing in it during the escape. I'd lost an awful lot of weight and was now very thin. (In compensation, my big breasts, which used to embarrass me so much that I would bind them, were now pleasingly small.) Finally my uncle produced some special *tsampa*, and I managed to eat it. Slowly I began to recover my strength and vitality.

I stayed with my great-uncle for a month, doing little except recuperate and play with Serkong Dorje Chang after he'd finished his lessons and said all his prayers. He was a plump, very happy child with enormous energy, unlike any four-year-old I had ever seen in that he actively seemed to enjoy the lessons my uncle gave him. Nor did he object to the strict discipline and rigorous schedule that he had to follow. In fact I noticed he was extremely diligent, even though he was so young, keen to learn and study as hard as he could. It was the first time I had witnessed a reincarnated lama and I was utterly fascinated. My uncle told me that this eagerness to learn was typical of all correctly identified reincarnated lamas. 'They have the imprints of the Buddha's teachings on their mind streams from all their previous lives and are in a hurry to develop them afresh. Normally all they have to do is hear them a few times before they know them. Sometimes they even begin to contradict the teacher,' he explained.

Serkong Dorje Chang could trace his incarnations back to the eleventh century in an unbroken wisdom lineage, even though he was now only four. Here, before my eyes, was an example of what Tibet was so famous for – conscious reincarnation, intriguing to outsiders but natural to us. In his last life Serkong Dorje Chang would have directed his consciousness at death precisely to a rebirth where he could continue to teach and guide others to find the way to everlasting peace and happiness. He had been doing this for a thousand years in Tibet, but now that religious freedom was profoundly curtailed in that country it made sense that he had chosen to be reborn in a country that was free. My uncle had the important job of training him to take up the mantle of his former position once more.

Serkong Dorje Chang also enjoyed playing with toys, the like of which I had never seen. I used to spend hours playing with him, loving every minute. Maybe I was making up for some of the fun I had missed out on during my own childhood.

My great-uncle was kind, respectable and extremely conventional. Like my father he had been brought up in the strict monastic tradition of old Tibet, where rigorous discipline was the order of the day. All his life he'd been surrounded exclusively by men, most of whom were monks, and I think he was utterly unnerved by having a young teenage girl in his house. In his eyes I was an enormous responsibility. When I had recovered and wanted to go out, he insisted I wore traditional Tibetan dress and had my hair plaited, so that I looked decent. I wanted to wear trousers or a skirt and yearned for my hair to hang loose. He was fearful for my reputation and nervous of my taking up with boys.

He need not have worried. I'd never had a boyfriend – I just didn't think that way. You're still considered a child in Tibet until you are 21. I didn't even have romantic thoughts. I'd never seen my mother and father sleeping together, I'd never even seen couples kissing. I was very shy about all of that. We were not exposed to sexuality in Tibet. You never saw couples embracing on the TV, on posters, or in magazines – that was decadent Western stuff. And my own life had been exceptionally closeted. All I knew was that you got married and then babies came, but I had no idea how. I was totally ignorant about the facts of life.

I had escaped from Tibet, I was safe, but my future was still very uncertain. My great-uncle suggested I could go to a private school in Kathmandu. He was a kind man and I appreciated enormously all he had done for me, but my mind was still set on the Dalai Lama. And I knew that if I stayed with my great-uncle my life would be bound by rules and restrictions once more. That wasn't what I had risked my life for. Politely I told him I preferred to go to Dharamsala in north India, to see the Dalai Lama, and that I would enrol in a school there. I think he was secretly relieved to see the back of me, because he didn't resist too much. He soon arranged for a respectable middle-aged Tibetan who was travelling to Dharamsala to take me with him, and in no time at all I was off, casting my fate to the winds and trusting in the protection of the Buddha. I was happy to be on my way again, travelling towards my dream, gambling yet once more.

We travelled by bus, traversing the high, green mountain ranges that separate Nepal from India. As I could speak neither Nepali nor Hindi I just observed. The scenery was breath-takingly beautiful, with high terraced fields and bushes of bright flowers. I watched horrified as tiny children tottered towards the edge of precipices, no one looking or preventing them from falling to their death. But they were quite safe. I guess they were used to living at that altitude. In Tibet no one lives perched on high mountain sides, except hermits in caves – we all stay in the valleys.

The bus broke down continually. We'd all pile out while the driver fixed it, and sit around drinking *chai*, sweet Indian milk tea flavoured with spices. I liked it a lot but I thought the tea sellers looked very poor – even poorer than people in Tibet. We passed several checkpoints where we had to pay a toll for using the road and we were cheated by being charged extra for the goods on the roof, which weren't ours.

We travelled south towards Delhi, our first stop. It was late at night when we finally juddered to a halt at the bus terminus. I looked through the window and gasped. The moon was hovering in the branches of a tree, close enough for me to climb up and touch it. How could this possibly be, I wondered. This miracle, I deduced, had to be a wonderful geographical feature that was something to do with India. Actually, it was a huge street-light – something I had never seen.

We put up in a hotel and the following night caught the bus north to Dharamsala in Himachal Pradesh, the most mountainous state of India. With dawn we began to climb out of the plains and up towards the mountains, to the former British hill station where the Dalai Lama and thousands of Tibetans have made their home. Snow appeared on distant mountain peaks. Gradually more Tibetans came into view and for the first time since leaving Tibet I began to feel excited. I'm getting closer and closer to the Dalai Lama, I thought.

For me, as for nearly every Tibetan, the Dalai Lama is more than just a good, wise, kind man. He is a living divinity – the emanation of the Buddha of Compassion, we believe, who walks this earth – and represents the soul of Tibet. Although he had been forced to leave the country long before I was born, his significance was embedded naturally in my very being. Since the invasion he had become a beacon of hope, burning brightly even in exile. He was alive, and so the true spirit of Tibet also lived.

I registered at the Exile Office where I gave my name simply as Soname. I wanted to forget Soname Yangchen, who belonged to another life. Besides, every time I heard someone say that name it reminded me of the Tashis ordering me about or scolding me. This was a new beginning, and it warranted a new identity.

I was taken to a guesthouse affiliated to one of the monasteries which had a very cheap, subsidised canteen. My great-uncle had given me money, but I had to watch every rupee. I sat down to a meal of *mo-mos*, and my rosy red cheeks – a dead giveaway that I had newly arrived from Tibet – soon attracted the attention of the other diners. They were eager to hear fresh news from home and the story of my escape. When I related all that had happened to me, they were surprised that the journey had been so smooth. For many the attempt had gone dreadfully wrong. I listened while they related their sad, harrowing tales.

There was the renowned sculptor who had made beautiful Buddha statues before he was set to work by the Chinese

making knives and spoons. Eventually he managed to escape
with his son, only for them both to be caught at the Nepalese
border, robbed of their few possessions, separated and thrown in
prison. After a long time in jail, the sculptor was released and
made his way to Dharamsala, where he now made exquisite statues for the Dalai Lama's temple, but he had no knowledge of
what had happened to his child.

Geography and the sheer brutality of the weather had
defeated many others. I heard of escapees who had edged along
tiny high rock ledges, only centimetres wide, their face to the
mountain, their arms outstretched, their feet at positioned at 'a
quarter to three', only to lose their footing and plunge thousands of feet to their death on the rocks below. Others had hung
upside down from broken rope suspension bridges, lost their
hold and been swept away by the furious waters while their
companions looked helplessly on. Many had been robbed and
abandoned by their paid guides in the middle of the night while
they slept and had been hopelessly lost for months in unknown
territory. Some had fallen down crevasses in the ice and never
been seen again. Others had simply frozen to death.

I learnt that each year different routes were taken out of
Tibet. Some went via the sacred mountain Kailash, in west
Tibet, others over the impossibly steep ranges towards Bhutan.
I realised that every single escapee diced with death in his or her
desperation to leave Tibet. For the first time it struck home how
incredibly fortunate I had been.

I found the bulk of the Tibetan community, including the
Dalai Lama's residence, in McLeod Ganj, a town above Dharamsala. It may have had an English church (where Lord Elgin was
buried) and a few remaining colonial bungalows, but to all
intents and purposes I had arrived in Little Lhasa. The main
street was divided by a row of prayer wheels, while Tibetans of
all shapes and sizes walked past and spun them. There were
Tibetan restaurants everywhere, some as small as shoe boxes,
selling Tibetan fare as well as chocolate cake, pizza and muesli
for the many Western tourists who flocked there having newly

discovered Buddhism. There were temples, monasteries, nunneries, with crowds of well-scrubbed monks and nuns all looking confident and happy.

Wandering around, I spotted schools for painting, metallurgy and woodwork. Master craftsmen and their apprentices beavered away inside, their subjects strictly religious. There was an academy for dance and theatre too. Down the hill were the impressive Tibetan Library and Archive, the government buildings, the hospital and medical school. The whole place was alive and buzzing with Tibetan culture and energy. What had been decimated in Tibet had been resurrected here.

I felt so proud. This was a tremendous achievement, a testimony to the resourcefulness, energy and determination of my people. I heard later that Dharamsala was the most successful refugee community in the world. At one stage during my preliminary exploration, I looked up and saw a flag fluttering on a nearby building. It depicted two deer standing beside the wheel of *dharma*. This was the flag of Tibet – and it was the first time in my life that I had seen it. Now you are truly free, I thought.

Three weeks later the day that I had dreamt of arrived. I was told that His Holiness the Dalai Lama was going to meet the new arrivals from Tibet, a practice he has kept up ever since he fled to India himself. As there has been a constant stream pouring over the border for more than 40 years, and as he talks to each one personally, this rite takes up a lot of his precious time. I put on the cleanest clothes I had, and with butterflies in my stomach made my way to the audience room. As I walked, I remembered how it was his name alone that had kept me going when I was escaping over the mountains. 'The Dalai Lama is waiting for you over the next peak,' Ngawang Panchen had said. Now that moment had actually come.

His Indian 'palace' was a far cry from the magnificence of the Potala in Lhasa, his previous home. It was a modest house with a view overlooking the mountains and a pretty garden kept by the Dalai Lama himself, who loves flowers. The audience room itself was very simple: there was a carpet on the floor, some

Tibetan *tangkas*, or cloth paintings, on the wall and an armchair for the Dalai Lama to sit on.

He walked in – and I couldn't see him. My head was down, my eyes blurred by tears. I was completely overcome, as was everybody else in the room. When I finally looked up I was mesmerised. The Dalai Lama was unlike any Tibetan I had ever seen. His skin was unusually white, unlike the brown skin normal for our race, and when he spoke his voice was extraordinary. I had been musical since childhood, with an ear attuned to the sounds of nature, able to pick up any song I heard, and I knew the Dalai Lama's voice was exceptional. It was strangely melodic, charming, utterly beautiful to listen to. My immediate reaction was that a man with a voice like this could never be harsh with women. It was a silly, romantic notion, that of an innocent young girl. I had no idea that the Dalai Lama was celibate. That was how little I knew about him.

He started to speak. He stated categorically that we now had our freedom. Hearing him say it endorsed all that we had endured. Then, like a father rather than a supreme spiritual and political leader, he began to give us advice, talking intimately. 'India is very different from Tibet,' he began. 'Because it is extremely hot you have to wash frequently, unlike in Tibet, so that you do not smell and cause offence. Also,' he went on, 'do not drink so much butter tea. The fat is bad for your health in this climate!'

Then he said, enigmatically: 'Do not forget the Chinese language because it might come in useful in the future.' What did he mean? The Dalai Lama had always told us to love our enemies, especially the Chinese, and had advocated a policy of non-violence, for which he was soon to be awarded the Nobel Peace Prize. Maybe he could see that his stance would eventually pay off and that one day Tibet and China would be on better terms.

The Dalai Lama was everything that I had ever expected, and more. To my mind there was no doubt that he was no ordinary man, but was indeed the emanation of the Buddha of Compassion. Every gesture he made was graceful, even when he scratched his bald head. And every one of us in that room, as well as the guards at the door, felt that he loved us unconditionally. We Tibetans call him Kundun, which means simply Presence, and all the time I was with him I knew I was in the presence of The Presence. I knew then with absolute certainty that everything I had risked in escaping had been worth it. In the Dalai Lama I had found a beacon of inspiration, and the epitome of what Tibet had once stood for.

CHAPTER NINE

Motherhood

IT WAS NOW EARLY 1989, and aged around 16, I went to school for the first time in my life, enrolling at a boarding school for older Tibetan girls in Biri, a hamlet down in the valley, a few hours by bus from Dharamsala. It was in a beautiful location, full of trees and Indian tea bushes, but the building itself was pretty basic. It consisted of just four rooms, with a tin roof that turned the classrooms into ovens during the long hot summer months. I was given toothpaste, soap, a plate, cup and spoon, and was shown to my bunk in a dormitory that held 25 girls.

Although my heart yearned for education, I was utterly hopeless. The problem was that I did not know how to study, the process of learning. I had never been taught this first rudimentary step. I only knew how to do physical work. The teacher would say 'Open the book at page such and such,' but even that was impossible for me. I didn't know the book and I didn't know the number.

I struggled to learn the Tibetan alphabet and when I managed to conquer a few words, I felt inordinately proud. We were also taught simple English – 'this is apple, this is airplane' – which thanks to my ear I mimicked, parrot fashion, quite successfully. Maths, however, was a complete disaster. I could not get my head around that at all. Anything to do with numbers or calculation has always been complete anathema to me. After a while I began to wish there was no need for reading and writing in the world, only the knowledge of how to say prayers. Wouldn't we all be happier that way? I seriously wondered if this education business was worth all the effort.

What I could do, however, was sing. I taught the other children the traditional songs my grandmother had taught me, how to project their voices, how to pitch. One day we heard that the Dalai Lama wanted to visit the school and it was decided that we should all sing to him. We did well, and when he beamed it was the proudest moment of my life.

A couple of months into my school life, just after the Tibetan New Year, I went to Dharamsala, along with the entire refugee community, to get a blessing from the Dalai Lama. There I bumped into a man whom I'd met when I first arrived. Tenzin was tall, slim and well educated. He wore glasses, was about 28 years old, and worked in the Tibetan Information Office translating documents from Chinese into Tibetan. He was from a good family, had been sent to China to be educated, and had escaped after returning to Tibet. His knowledge of both Tibet and China was invaluable. He said he was having a party that night. Lots of friends would be there and there would be *momos* to eat. Would I come?

I had a great time – there was music, singing and dancing. But when it was time to go home it was pouring with rain and the streets and gutters were like rivers. Nowhere does it rain as heavily as it does in Dharamsala! In fact, Dharamsala has the dubious honour of being the wettest town in the whole of India, which was why it was given to the Dalai Lama when he sought refuge. Basically, no one else wanted to live in the damp, deserted former British hill station. There was no way I could get back to the school and Tenzin suggested I should stay. He had two single beds, which reassured me. With no other option, I accepted.

During the night, however, he came into my bed saying he was cold. He started touching me and forcing himself on me. Being so naïve, I didn't really understand what was happening, but I felt powerless – and besides I had nowhere to run. Whatever he was doing, I hated it. Tibetan men generally know nothing about romance and gentleness. It isn't their way. They are earthy and wild, like their country, and when they feel attracted to a woman they often do away with the preliminaries and simply try and jump on her. This was my introduction to sex (I couldn't call it making love). There was nothing pleasurable about it – in fact it hurt like hell, as if chillies were burning inside me. In the morning, depressed and sore, I went back to school.

I didn't take much notice when I missed a period, but when I stopped feeling hungry and wanting to eat, I began to get concerned. I noticed my breasts becoming bigger and getting a little sore and then I started vomiting. Convinced I had contracted some dreadful illness, I went to the hospital to find out what was wrong. The doctor examined me and announced I was pregnant. At his words my heart dropped about five metres. This was the last thing I had expected, a calamity so enormous that I could hardly take it in.

I went back to school, scared out of my mind. I knew now where babies came from. To my horror I was about to have a 'bastard', the insult that had followed me during childhood in Yarlung. The shock and shame I felt was unbearable. I could not focus on my studies and did not dare tell anyone. I did not know what to do. I was still a young girl, alone in India, with no education, no husband, no family, no job, and I was about to have a baby. How was I going to survive? How was my child going to survive? My karma must be really negative, I thought, to have managed to escape, to have endured so much to gain freedom, only to end up trapped in this appalling predicament. My liberty had been short lived.

I hadn't seen Tenzin since the night of the party but in desperation I wrote to tell him the news, and to my surprise he turned up at school. 'No problem! You can come and live with me. I like you a lot – and have done since I first met you,' he said breezily. I had no idea how it would work out, but at least it was a solution, if only for the time being.

And so my all too brief education came to an abrupt halt, and I was jettisoned into the role of an exceedingly young house-wife and expectant mother. I moved into his room, provided by the government. It was abysmally basic. Apart from the two beds it contained a kerosene stove with one burner, a tiny table and a small borrowed music player which only sometimes worked. That was it. Our Dharamsala community may have been remarkably successful but we were still refugees with colossal problems to overcome.

But Tenzin seemed to be basically a kind man, ready to help those in need and utterly dedicated to the Tibetan cause. We were never officially married but in my mind he was my hus-band and I was his wife. We were dirt poor. Tenzin's salary was a mere 500 rupees a month, which he handed over to me. I eked it out so that we had enough to eat – just. I tried cooking on the tiny stove but successfully managed to burn everything, the result of never having learned to cook, and so most of the time we ate in the canteen, which worked out cheaper than buying food and fuel for the stove anyway.

Strangely enough, I became happy living with Tenzin. I even learnt to love him – and I felt he did me. We certainly had fun together. We laughed and played together like children. He gave me lessons in how to read and write Tibetan. Sometimes we paid two rupees to watch English videos in little restaurants. I would spend the whole time whispering, 'What are they say-ing?' and Tenzin would try and translate, although his English was not much better than mine. Our main entertainment, how-ever, was doing *cora* of Dharamsala's many religious sites, Tenzin taking my hand as we walked around the holy objects, saying mantras and accumulating good karma.

My pregnancy progressed uneventfully, even though I had no idea what was in store, no mother to turn to for advice, no one other than Tenzin for support. After the first few weeks I stopped vomiting and felt fine, though Tenzin started feeling sick instead, as if by proxy. Aware that I was very small in stature, I tried to look more adult, as befitted my new status and pending motherhood, by wearing high heels and long jackets. Not that it mattered, because until the last few weeks I never looked pregnant, and nobody knew. For some reason my baby hid itself and my stomach stayed flat. I did not even have stretch marks.

Because I was small and Tibetan babies are notoriously big – especially their heads – the doctor told me to get plenty of exercise, as this would reduce the baby's size and make the birth easier. It was an easy order to follow. Dharamsala is perched on the side of a steep mountain and I got plenty of exercise just stepping outside my front door.

I knew absolutely nothing about childbirth, and I don't think many other young Tibetan girls of my acquaintance did either. It is a curious feature of our culture that although our women are famously independent and feisty, we balk at discussing the details of birth. In our society it simply isn't done. I remember, when I was very small, asking my mother where babies came from and she indicated her armpit. This ignorance does not serve us well. For instance, I had got it into my head that pregnancies lasted a year. I went only once to the hospital for a check-up, and when the nurse asked me how pregnant I was, I answered, 'Eleven months.' 'That's not possible!' the nurse replied. I was always hopeless with numbers.

So when the baby started coming I was taken completely unawares. The pains started in the middle of the night and I began to lose blood, which I thought was part of the natural process. I didn't want to disturb Tenzin, who was sleeping, so I found a green plastic bucket, thinking the baby would drop into that with no trouble at all. I got some cloth ready to wrap it in and believed that would be that. I had no idea there was a cord to cut and an afterbirth to be delivered. I knew my mother had given birth at home and I thought I would follow suit. I'd seen animals give birth when I was growing up in the country and as far as I could remember they didn't seem to have too much trouble. They simply dropped them on the ground – just as I was going to do.

For all my squatting over the bucket, however, the baby didn't appear. The pain became much worse and I conceded I probably needed help. I shook my husband. 'Wake up! The baby is coming,' I said. Tenzin was out of bed in a flash and out the door. He returned with his friend and wife, who was already a mother, and together we set off on foot to the hospital, which was about 15 minutes away. None of us had a car and there was no way we could afford a taxi.

During the walk the pain was excruciating. Every time I had a contraction my knees buckled and I dropped to the road. Tenzin and his friends helped me up again and we continued to walk slowly on, until the next contraction when I'd fall again. But finally I reached the hospital where I was checked in. For the next two days the labour continued, but still no baby.

I could not stand the disinfectant smell of the hospital – it made my eyes sting – and as no baby was forthcoming, I walked back up the hill to our room. Then the contractions started again so I returned to the hospital. I made that journey three times, with the pain intensifying all the time. The pain was terrible. My back ached continuously, and the backache was as bad as the contractions. The only way I could relieve it was by leaning heavily into a hard tin chest. Tenzin was with me all the time, holding my hand. He smoked so many cigarettes that his tongue went numb.

It was a very difficult birth. I was bleeding heavily now and was sure the baby was dead. Still, I can't say I was frightened. I had never been afraid of dying, not when I ran away as a child, not during my escape, and not now when I was having a baby. My whole life had been a gamble. What did I have to lose? If I die, I die, I thought. After a week of hard, agonising labour I made my last trip to the hospital and my baby finally entered the world, sliding out of me fast, like a hot fish.

My daughter was born on 18 March 1990. It is the only date

in my entire life that I am absolutely sure about because the doctor wrote it down. She was absolutely beautiful and I fell instantly in love with her. Before putting her to the breast I did what every Tibetan woman does – I gave her a little butter to suck. This, we believe, helps moisturise the baby's stomach, lessens the acidity of the milk and helps reduce the pain of digestion. Butter is the cure for everything!

The butter may have helped her in the feeding process but for me it was an excruciatingly painful exercise because she sucked so hard. But I persevered and continued to feed her, which was just as well since we could not afford powdered milk. She was named by the Dalai Lama. Every New Year he writes names on slips of paper for babies born at that time and we went to the administration office to choose one – Deckyi, which means Happiness.

If I were at home in Yarlung I would have been put to bed for a month after giving birth, and fed chicken soup to build up my strength and restore my muscles while the family did the chores and looked after the baby. As a displaced person living in a refugee community this was impossible, of course, and I had to fend for myself with my newborn babe as well as I could. Although we were living in one room with hardly enough to eat, the next few months were surprisingly happy. Deckyi was the cutest baby ever, so pretty that everybody loved her. I had such fun playing with her – I had never been concerned with maintaining an air of decorum and anyway I was not much more than a girl myself.

Her father and I were getting on well. We both doted on the baby and took enormous interest in everything she did. I was woefully ignorant about what was needed in looking after a baby, but a friendly neighbour came in and taught me the practical steps. Even so, one day when I was washing her she became so slippery with soap that she slid out of my hands into the bath and swallowed lots of water. I panicked, picked her up and ran with her to the hospital. 'My baby has drowned!' I shouted at the nurse. She took one look at Deckyi and replied, 'The baby's fine, go home.' When I told Tenzin that night, he just said 'Bloody hell!' He was a good father and he loved us both a lot, I thought.

I imagined that we would go on in the same way for ever – living in Dharamsala, bringing up Deckyi. I felt settled and happy, enjoying the family life that had been denied me so long. This was what I had been yearning for during all my years with the Tashis in Lhasa. Unbeknown to me, however, our poverty was grinding Tenzin down. One day, while I was pegging out nappies on the clothes line, he came to me and said almost casu-ally, 'Come inside and sit down, I've got something to tell you. There is a chance that I may be sponsored to get an education in New York.' He would be away for two years, he said, during which time he could save and come back with enough money to set us up.

I went cold inside. What he was saying was threatening to break apart my new-found security. In my head I realised there was sense in what he was suggesting: an offer like this did not come every day and would definitely improve his career as well as helping us financially. With English under his belt, as well as Tibetan and Chinese, his prospects would be much better. But my heart said, 'Don't go, don't leave me alone with a baby.' I didn't voice my feelings, but I hoped in my heart that the offer would come to nothing.

Over the next few weeks he talked about New York with increasing regularity and certainty. Finally he told me he was definitely going. 'Things aren't getting any better here. My salary can hardly feed two of us. When Deckyi gets a little older I won't have enough,' he said. I wanted to be a good wife and support him, and I felt I could last two years. 'Well, if it gives you more power to work for the Tibetan cause, then you should go. It will be good for all of us,' I replied bravely. Still, I was very sad. We hadn't been apart for a day since I'd moved in with him and he was the closest person to me now in the world, apart from my daughter. I felt I was losing not just my husband, but my friend, mother and father too.

He left carrying a change of trousers and a shirt in a borrowed suitcase. Before he went he had given me all the money he could muster, 3,000 rupees, leaving practically nothing for himself. When he finally walked out of the door I was devastated. It was another wrench, another goodbye, another upheaval.

No matter what you want, if you don't have the karma it will not happen regardless of whether you are rich or poor. That is the spiritual way of thinking, and it was what I told myself. But there was an ordinary voice saying in the other ear, 'You and your daughter have been abandoned.' Deckyi was just 11 months old and I was alone against the world once more, with no idea what lay in store. I had heard that in the West women were very free sexually and that marriages only lasted a few months before couples got divorced and started sleeping around again, and I did not think Tenzin would last long. Something in me said that once he had walked out of the door I would never see him again.

CHAPTER TEN

The Abyss

ECKYI AND I MANAGED to get along alone for about a year, fortified by the thought that Tenzin would be returning in the not too distant future. He wrote to me occasionally, telling me that he was well and doing fine in New York. Then, after 12 months, the 3,000 rupees that he had given me finally ran out and I knew I had to get a job.

After a long day trudging around Dharamsala I finally found employment packing incense in a small Tibetan cottage industry. All went smoothly while Deckyi was still little. But soon she began crawling, then walking, picking up everything she came across and putting it in her mouth – even dead spiders. I was completely distracted. My fellow workers began to complain: 'You're always watching the child and not pulling your weight.' Soon I was asked to leave.

Things were not going well. One day I bumped into one of Tenzin's friends, who announced bluntly, 'Your husband's written to say that New York is paradise, he is doing good work for the Tibetan cause, and please would I keep an eye on you and your daughter because he is not coming back.' I stood there in the street, mouth open, dumbfounded. I was absolutely shattered. I didn't know what to think. New York was obviously dazzling, far more exciting than Deckyi or me. Or perhaps he had been caught by one of the promiscuous American girls I had heard of. Whatever the reason, I felt completely betrayed. What made it worse was that I had had to hear it from a third party. Tenzin did not even have the guts to tell me himself.

I struggled on, living on practically nothing, my life uncertain, feeling dreadfully alone. Thankfully I had a few friends who I could talk to, and they were a great comfort to me. One of them was a man from the Tibetan province of Amdo who had a high position in the Tibetan government. I used to go to his place in the evening to eat, taking Deckyi with me. I had picked up a little Chinese during my Lhasa days when I used to bargain with the Chinese merchants around the Barkhor and listen to the Chinese radio programmes, and we both liked to practise our Chinese together as the Dalai Lama had recommended. We would reminisce about life in Tibet and compare it to our new existence in Dharamsala.

The man from Amdo was good with Deckyi, picking her up when she cried and making a fuss of her. That was wonderful for me to see. I worried that there wasn't a male presence in Deckyi's life: every child should be able to say 'Daddy' as well as 'Mummy', I thought. It was a good friendship. But gradually – whether it was loneliness, I don't know, or the fact that I became aware he was attracted to me – our relationship began to change. We became closer until the friendship became an affair.

I knew now that Tenzin was not coming back, and I desperately needed emotional and physical support. This man was handsome, intelligent, and kind to Deckyi, while I was sad and lonely. I let go and fell in love, praying with all my heart that he and I would get married. My lover healed a lot of my pain, restored my badly dented self-esteem and confidence, but I soon began to see that our relationship was not going the way I hoped. He never told me he loved me or needed me, never suggested we make it permanent. He would not even let me move in with him. In fact he wanted to keep our liaison absolutely secret. 'No one must know,' he said.

Slowly I began to understand. Yes, he found me physically attractive, but I was not the wife he had in mind. He was extremely ambitious and wanted a wife who was educated, who could speak English fluently and be an asset to his career. I did not fit the bill. In fact, in contrast to the infinitely freer sexual mores of Tibet, affairs were frowned upon in Dharamsala. Tibetans in exile had become very conservative, conscious of the image they presented to the outside world. Here everything had to be impeccable and above board. Dharamsala was a holy place, they reasoned, where the Dalai Lama lived. They wanted everything to appear 'pure'. Personally I found this attitude ridiculous and I hated the hypocrisy.

Of course, gradually people came to know about our relationship because they saw me going to his house. All too soon our affair became a big scandal in that small, tightly knit community. Gossip raged around Dharamsala like wildfire and rapidly my reputation lay in tatters. People would smile and whisper as I walked past. It was horrible − I knew they were looking down on me, saying vile things.

None of this would have happened if I had been back in Tibet. My family would have pleaded my cause, defended my honour and arranged a marriage. But here I had no one to defend me. As my name became blacker and the scandal more virulent, my lover did not stand by me. He was far too busy guarding his own reputation. With remarkable speed, he dropped me.

I was shattered at being abandoned yet again. Now, two men whom I had trusted had walked out on Deckyi and me, leaving us to fend for ourselves. What had I done to deserve this, I wondered. Part of me bitterly regretted starting the affair, but a small part also knew that what I had done was completely in character. I had always been headstrong, spontaneous, fearless, plunging in wherever my heart would lead me, not thinking about the consequences. That's how I had escaped from Tibet. Besides, I was in love with the man from Amdo (although in retrospect I do not think I really loved him), I needed the comfort he gave me. I tried to muster my old resilient self, and those feisty independent Tibetan female genes. I can face the world without a man to protect me, I thought. I will survive, and my daughter will survive too. After all, how much worse can it get, I wondered. I had only to wait.

Within days I was given notice that I had to get out of our room since it was allotted for government workers only. As my husband was not coming back and there was someone else who qualified for the room I had to vacate. Now I was truly cornered. I had nowhere to go, no one to turn to, no job, no money. I began to panic. How on earth was I going to look after Deckyi? I was facing destitution.

To my shame I was not coping with Deckyi as well as I hoped. Every day she was becoming more demanding and my emotional state was becoming increasingly frayed. Being alone with a small child is awful – when you are broke and facing homelessness too it is traumatic beyond description. *Please help me*, I prayed to the Buddha, *I don't think I can go on.*

It seemed at first that the Buddha must still be looking down on me. Next day on the street I bumped into a friend of Tenzin's with some strangers. When he introduced us I found to my amazement that they were Tenzin's parents, newly arrived in Dharamsala from Tibet having been granted travel papers to come to India on pilgrimage to visit the major Buddhist sacred sites. They had learnt that their son had had a child, and the meeting was extremely cool, to say the least. They didn't ask how I was or engage in polite conversation. They must have heard the rumours, I thought, and disapprove of me. They think I'm an unsuitable mother for their grandchild.

They certainly knew about my dire situation. After two or three days they sent a message asking me to meet them in a restaurant, where they put forward a plan: 'It's clear you can't look after Deckyi. We will take her with us to Tibet and bring her up there. After a few years she can come back to you. By that time your life will be more settled.' It was an appalling suggestion. How could I possibly let my daughter go? But I was desperate, down to my last few rupees. Maybe this was the solution, the answer to my cry to the Buddha. I told Deckyi's grandparents I would go away and think about it.

If I thought of Deckyi rather than myself I knew that she would have a better life with her grandparents. At least these people were her relatives, I reasoned, they were able to look after her, which was more than I could do. Within Dharamsala I was blacklisted, a fallen woman with no future at all. I deliberated all night, unable to think straight. In the end I decided I had no choice. I had to give Deckyi up for her own sake. The decision filled me with terrible despair and inexpressible guilt. I was doing to her what had been done to me, only at a much younger age. Will she ever forgive me, I agonised, will she ever understand?

With an aching heart, I told Tenzin's parents of my decision. They told me they were leaving for Tibet from Delhi, and I borrowed 1,000 rupees in order to travel with them, in order to be with Deckyi for as long as I could. They planned to be in Delhi for one week, but I could only afford to book into a hotel for one night – I wanted to give Deckyi as much money as I could when she left. Without telling them, or the hotel staff, after everyone had gone to bed I would sneak up to the flat roof and spend the entire night there with Deckyi lying on my lap. The noise was incredible: traffic went past all night, planes flew overhead and the whine of mosquitoes buzzed in my ears. I got bitten half to death, but made sure I kept Deckyi covered.

In the morning I would creep down to the restaurant with Deckyi, wash our faces and hands in the bathroom, and have a cup of tea as though we had spent a comfortable night in bed. The poor are desperate to maintain their dignity, and I was no exception. I wanted to keep up appearances as well as I could and did not want to be more humiliated than I felt already in front of Tenzin's parents.

Knowing I was letting my daughter go, those last few days were sheer torture. I kept staring at her all the time, trying to imprint every expression of her face on my mind. We took photographs with a camera that a friend had leant me in a futile attempt to capture her presence. Every single second with her was precious. Finally the day came for her to leave. I kissed her and held her to me, before giving her grandparents my last 500 rupees. 'If she needs some milk or some food, please buy it for her,' I begged. It was the only thing left for me to do. 'Please, can I get someone to write for me and let me know how Deckyi is.'

They looked at me stony faced. 'It's better for her that there is no contact. That way she will settle down more easily,' they replied. And the way they looked told me that they felt Deckyi was better off without me. In their eyes I was a fallen woman, and Deckyi would have a better chance of growing up with me out of the picture entirely.

I was so stunned I said nothing. Now I can see that I was so utterly conditioned to obeying my elders without question that it never occurred to me to protest. What was more, a small part of me believed they might be right. Besides, what could I do? I couldn't snatch her back. I still had no money to feed her. And so they took her away. I watched while the bus disappeared into the distance, every sinew of my body wanting to race after it. I would have chased after it in another bus if I could, but I didn't have a single rupee left.

After she had gone I fell into an abyss. I wandered aimlessly around Delhi, crying, crying. I slept on the streets like a beggar. It was winter and the streets were cold, but I did not care. I was numb, riddled with guilt, my heart torn apart. What had I done? I should never have let her go, I told myself over and over again.

At some point, I don't know how, I found myself at Majnu Katilla, the Tibetan colony in Delhi, in a restaurant run by a Tibetan monk. He took one look at me, sat me down, and gave me a cup of tea. Faced with his kindness, I poured out what had happened. He said in a gentle voice: 'Don't cry and don't worry. It will all work out OK. Your daughter is safe. Now you must look for a job or resume your studies. Go back to our people in Dharamsala, where you will feel more at home.' And he gave me 200 rupees for a third-class bus fare back to where I had come from.

The bus was full of Indian village people, and it stopped everywhere. I didn't care. I was in a world of my own. My heart had turned cold, my mind was not working properly, and I could not stop crying. I was aware of a kind Indian woman sitting next to me who wanted to know what was wrong. She thought my mother had died. But I couldn't speak, I couldn't utter a word.

When I got back to my rented room, which I had not yet vacated, and opened the door, the first thing my eyes fell on were Deckyi's clothes strewn over the floor. I picked them up. Her smell was still on them. That was the final straw. I collapsed on the bed and burst into uncontrollable sobs. My whole body, my whole being, was racked with unbearable pain. I stayed on that bed for the next week unable to stop weeping, unable to go out, unable to eat, unable to sleep. My innate strength had left me completely. I missed my daughter beyond words and my guilt was as big as the mountain I had climbed. How could I go on living when I had abandoned this vulnerable, helpless person who was part of my soul and the meaning of my life?

With Deckyi gone and all my dreams smashed I did not care whether I lived or died. My despair was fathomless. Thoughts of killing myself began to come into my head. I could see no point in living any more. I knew suicide was strictly against the Buddhist religion, because life is deemed precious and one has to live out one's karma, but I was past caring. What did it matter? I would probably go to hell anyway for being an abnormal mother who had abandoned her child.

A neighbour found me and tried to rouse me. 'What are you doing? It's like cursing your daughter, crying like this. Stop it,' he said, sternly but kindly. 'Your daughter is fine. Of course she misses you a little but she is OK. You did what you had to do, you had no choice. You were doing the best for your daughter.'

Every day he talked to me like that. He brought me *tsampa* to eat and hot sweet tea to drink. In effect he saved my life. Slowly, over several days, I clambered out of the dark pit I had fallen

into, and decided I had to go on living, for Deckyi's sake if not
my own. I realised I had to be around for her when she was
returned to Dharamsala as her grandparents had promised.

My first step was to get work. I owed my new landlady rent,
I had to eat, and I needed something to do to keep my mind off
Deckyi. I knew it would be easier without a small child to look
after. I traipsed around the many hotels in Dharamsala asking for
housekeeping work, the only skill I had. After a long day I finally
found a job in an Indian hotel catering for pilgrims and tourists.
The salary was 500 rupees a month, plus breakfast, lunch and
dinner. It was hardly anything, but it would pay for my rent, and
it was secure.

I could hardly believe how easy the work was – it was nothing compared to what I had to do as a child back in Lhasa. My
duties consisted of stripping and making the beds, putting the
dirty cups and plates outside the door, and dusting. That was it.
Sweeping, and cleaning the bathrooms – the 'dirty' jobs – were
left to the lower-caste Hindu staff. Coming from Tibet, the
Indian caste system was strange and abhorrent to me. I couldn't
understand why everyone didn't chip in and share the work as
we did back home. When no one was looking I used to help the
Hindu staff, like Ramesh, a sweet boy who was always smiling.
I would do the sweeping with him and tell him to serve himself
before me in the kitchen. No one had treated him like this
before and he became a good friend.

All the work was done by 1 pm but since I had to stay until
6.30 my fellow housemaids and I used to find an empty room
where we would watch cable TV, chat, and sneak hot showers.
These were a real luxury – no Tibetan refugee could afford such
opulence. We used to take turns watching out for the manager.

Even though I had no spare money, the work served the purpose of distracting me from dwelling on Deckyi all the time. In
quiet moments, however, thoughts of her came flooding back. I
missed her inordinately and the guilt still tore into me. I wondered how she was, if she were coping without me in a strange
land, if her relatives were being kind to her. I had not heard a

single word from them since she left. All I could do was make a little altar in my room and put Deckyi's photograph on it, next to a picture of the Buddha so that he could bless her.

Every day, before I went to work and when I came home, I prayed to the Buddha to please take care of my child. When her birthday came around I lit candles for her and offered her sweets on my altar. And whenever the despair threatened to engulf me again, I had learnt the trick of going to the local hospital to visit people worse off than myself. It's an old Buddhist remedy to make you feel better and to stop yourself sliding into self-pity. It worked, but only up to a point. At least, I reasoned, I was now functioning.

If I had found a job that was serving its purpose, my living arrangements were far from satisfactory. My landlady was extremely mean. She would not allow me to use electricity, except for the light bulb, which meant I had to hide my kettle from her when I wanted a cup of tea. She put a lock on the cold water tap outside my door, forcing me to fetch water from far away, and she locked the toilet too, making me trek to the public lavatory, as I had to do back in Tibet. This was a real nuisance, especially in the cold, snow-bound winter, or if I had caught one of India's many stomach bugs.

I stuck it out for a year until she announced she was putting the rent up. Then I had had enough. I moved in with a man called Tenzin Tsering who let rooms in his house. He charged only 200 rupees a month, which left me 300 rupees spending money – sheer wealth by my standards. He was an elderly Tibetan who had retired from the Indian army and we got on well. Of course, in that small community the tongues started wagging again, feeding on my already tarnished reputation. Rumours flew that we were having an affair, which was absurd. Dharamsala could be so small minded. Tenzin Tsering was very kind man, who cared about my welfare, and I liked him – that was all. We would sit and drink tea together, and talk about religion. I used to call him 'Father', which pleased me, as I'd never been close to an elderly man. I think he liked it too. As for my real father, I had no idea how he was. I hadn't heard from him, or from any other family member, since arriving in India, although I had written to tell my father where I was and that I was OK.

You cannot live in Dharamsala with the Dalai Lama as your neighbour without being affected. An aura of spirituality hangs in the air, and you breathe it in whether you mean to or not. Thousands of eager young monks dash about, learning their scriptures, energetically debating points of philosophy and saying their prayers. Artists and sculptors are busy creating beautiful Buddhist paintings and statues. Prayer wheels spin. Sacred texts are read. There are even yogis hidden in the hills above the main town, silently beaming out their meditations like lighthouses in this dark world, helping the Dalai Lama with his mission to bring peace to all.

In fact, I managed to find my own guru, a wrinkled old yogi with tattered robes and matted hair, who had spent much of his life in the mountains. He hadn't washed much during that life, because he was rather smelly, but I didn't mind. I have always believed that you should never judge anyone by their appearance, as you never know who they really are. The lowliest street person may be a Buddha.

I used to visit the yogi's ramshackle hut, balanced precariously on the hillside. It had a tin roof and a dirt floor, with a wooden pallet for a bed and a few tins of food stacked up in a corner. He didn't say much, but he seemed to know my heart. I would sit in front of him on the dirt floor while he prayed for me and my daughter, and when I left him I always felt uplifted, as though I wasn't the most wicked woman in the universe after all. One day he handed me a red blessing cord. I hung it around my neck and never took it off. In my darkest moments, when I was tortured over letting my daughter go and the abyss beckoned, I would hold it, addressing my thoughts and prayers to it. I felt that my yogi was picking them up via the cord, like a telephone wire, hearing my pleas and my anguish. I would imagine a cloak of protection falling over my daughter and me.

My kind landlord also encouraged my spiritual education. In 1994 the Dalai Lama was to give a high initiation, the Kalachakra, in Spiti, a remote region in the Indian Himalaya that borders Tibet. Tenzin Tsering urged me to go. 'This is a unique opportunity, and you should take it,' he explained. 'The Kalachakra is an extremely special initiation which promotes peace within the individual and through that, peace to the world at large. Kalachakra means "wheel of time". It refers both to the inner wheel of time – the movement of our breath and the various changes that take place within our body, and the outer wheel of time – the movements of the planets that make up this universe. It is prophesied that those who have taken the Kalachakra will find themselves reborn eventually in Shambhala, the Golden Age for the entire planet, when peace and loving-kindness shall reign supreme.

'This is the only Dalai Lama who has conferred the initiation upon the public at large. You have to go. I will give you money for the journey and for your board while you are there.' He generously handed me 3,000 rupees. I was moved, but said, 'I can get by on 2,000.' I gave him back the rest.

However, I met with a stony response from the hotel manager. He told me I could not take the time off: 'You have to choose between your job and this trip.' 'Well, this is the experience of a lifetime, so I choose the Kalachakra,' I replied. The boss was shocked, and so was I. In my precarious situation it was an enormous gamble for me to take. My boldness had obviously come back.

I went to Spiti with a girlfriend, Dolma, travelling in a rickety old tin bus crammed full of Tibetan pilgrims. The bus set off at an alarming rate, swerving around the hairpin bends all along the route. I looked out of the window and saw to my horror that our tyres were mere inches from the verge, with no barrier to stop us plunging over the edge to the rocks far below. Yet the driver seemed unconcerned. In fact spirits were high and we all sang at the tops of our voices.

After a day's bumpy, happy ride we arrived at Manali, the

town sitting at the base of the treacherous Rhotang Pass which guards the way to Spiti, another swerving bus-ride away. At nearly 4,000 metres, it's passable only during a few months in summer. For the rest of the year Spiti is cut off from the world by an impenetrable barrier of snow and ice. The area has been steeped in Buddhism for centuries, ever since thousands of Indian Buddhist monks fled to its hidden peaks from the persecution of the Moghul invasion.

Seeing thousands of maroon and gold robes lined up in front of the Dalai Lama in the midst of those spectacular high snow-capped mountains was the most fabulous sight. But what can I say about the initiation itself? Only that it was extremely esoteric and complex, and that it lasted for several days. I can't say I understood it. The Dalai Lama sat up front dressed in ornate robes, orchestrating the entire event. There were words we had to repeat after him, red ribbons to put over our eyes (representing a blindfold), prayers and mantras to say. At one point, armies of young monks dashed up and down the rows, giving everyone tea from immense silver teapots. And all the time we were aware of another circle of monks, bent over making an exquisite, intricate coloured mandala from grains of sand, representing the utopia of Shambhala.

Although the initiation went right over my head, I did feel *something*. Whatever the Dalai Lama was doing for all those days filled the atmosphere with a powerful, benign force that affected me deeply. At the end I took the lay person's vows – promising not to steal, not to take life and not to engage in sexual misconduct, which means not causing harm by coming between couples. I felt I had been truly blessed.

After 15 days it was back to Dharamsala where, of course, I had lost my job. I tried, but I couldn't find another one. Dolma, who had stayed in Manali after the Kalachakra and found a position as a housemaid in one of its many hotels, said there was a vacancy for me, and so I decided to join her. I was on the move once more, going to yet another new place to try my fortune. I got the job, moved into Dolma's room in the hotel and for the first time in many years began to have fun.

Manali is a thriving town, at the end of the beautiful Kulu Valley, with the gushing Beas River running through it, famed for its orchards and exquisite hand-crafted shawls. It was full of young Westerners discovering India and making their way to Ladakh, beyond Spiti in the Indian Himalayas. I noticed many Israelis there, unwinding after their military service. I myself was relieved to be away from Dharamsala, where I had experienced so much trauma and unhappiness. I began to feel free. I wasn't starving, I had a place to live, I was not in a destructive relationship, I had got over the man from Amdo, I had forgotten Tenzin, I was not worried sick about feeding a child. For the first time in my life it felt good to be a young woman tasting independence.

After work Dolma and I used to dress up and dance Western style in our room to Michael Jackson, my favourite, and Bob Marley. We couldn't afford to go to the nightclubs. We befriended a third girl who worked with us and whose life was even more difficult than ours. She had three children and her husband, a taxi driver, used to beat and rape her. He would take her earnings to buy drink, leaving her with nothing to feed her children properly. Dolma and I managed give her 100 rupees out of our 500-rupee salary to help her out. I knew more than anyone what it felt like to be absolutely dirt poor.

I really enjoyed myself during those summer months in Manali, but when winter came, life became tough. The temperature plummeted, the snow was waist high, and there was no heating in the hotel. Dolma and I would snuggle down in bed together to keep from freezing. Gradually the tourists stopped coming and the hotel closed.

I was out of a job again. I couldn't face going back to Dharamsala, but where could I go? What could I do? I'll try my luck in Delhi, I thought, it has plenty of hotels that are bound to need housekeepers. Once more, trusting that the Buddha would look after me, I stepped on to a bus and into the void.

CHAPTER ELEVEN

The Tide Turns

THE BUS FROM DHARAMSALA dropped me near the centre of Delhi in the late afternoon. With nowhere specifically to go and nothing particular to do, I headed for a park a little way off and sat down on a bench. I was quite relaxed, not at all worried about the blank slate that was my future. After what I had been through, I knew I could survive anything. What was there to be scared of in Delhi anyway? There were no secret police, no treacherous mountains to climb in the dark, no wild animals, no small child with an empty stomach to fill. There was only myself to worry about.

I was sitting there, happily watching people eat ice cream and listening to the sound of a fountain, when a woman in a red sari came and sat next to me. We started to chat in Hindi, which I'd managed to pick up, along with rudimentary English, while working with Indians and tourists in Dharamsala. 'Are you Japanese?' she asked. 'No, I'm Tibetan. I've just arrived in Delhi looking for work,' I answered. We talked on and I told her a little about myself, relating some of my adventures. I spoke honestly from my heart as I do with everyone I meet. She listened, absolutely rapt, and then said, 'Well, my sister is looking for staff to help her in her sari shop. I work there, but she needs someone else too. I'm sure you're more than capable. And, if you like, you can share my flat until you get sorted out.' It was a magnanimous gesture, the kind that can happen in India. My fairy godmother had arrived.

Her name was Lavina. She was 27 years old and had recently walked out on her alcoholic husband in Kerala, south India, leaving all her jewellery and possessions behind – including her business, a beauty parlour. It was a brave, radical move. To be single at her age in her culture was tremendously challenging. Lavina was bubbly, outgoing, cute looking and very Westernised (at least to my eyes), and she was to transform my life in a way I could never imagine.

She may have been a stranger whom I met during a chance encounter on a park bench, but I trusted her. I take people as I find them, I really don't care what their status is, or what they have done with their lives. And so I gratefully accepted Lavina's invitation to stay. I moved into her small third-floor flat near the centre of Delhi and began building up my life from scratch yet again, in a different city, a different culture, among different people.

My first hurdle was getting used to the strong, foreign cooking smells that pervaded the whole block of flats 24 hours a day. I didn't know how I was going to live with them. But after a few days I found I had got used to them, and after that I didn't notice them at all. I liked my Indian neighbours a lot. They were friendly and often asked me in for a cup of tea. I was happy to find myself in such a welcoming community, free from my past.

The Delhi heat, especially in summer, was not so easy to adapt to. Outside, it was almost intolerable for me. Inside, I was fortunate to have air conditioning, but still my body found it hard to cope with the drastic contrast in temperatures and I developed flu-like symptoms as a result. What's more, the air conditioning would regularly shut down due to Delhi's frequent power cuts, and then I'd open the window and be eaten alive by swarms of mosquitoes.

The heat was far worse for the poor on the streets, however

– for them it was literally a killer. Thousands died every year. When I first arrived the plight of the poor broke my heart.

I began work in the sari shop. My days were long, starting at 10 am and finishing at 10 pm, or later if there were customers in the shop. My wages were 2,000 rupees a month and I paid 1,000 rupees in rent (which was exorbitant by my standards), but I still had a little left over for spending money and food. Lavina's sister, Shiri, was wonderful and I admired her enormously. She was a determined, well-travelled woman who had started selling saris from her home and had built up her business until she owned this shop in a wealthy quarter of Delhi. She had all the drive and ambition in her family – her husband was useless, although extremely kind. Both of them treated me like a family member, taking me home at lunchtime to eat with them and their children. It was a stark contrast to my days as a child slave in Lhasa.

Gradually I began to learn the intricacies of sari selling. Shiri was extremely patient, teaching me about the exquisite fabrics, their different qualities and places of manufacture. No matter how I tried, though, I was absolutely hopeless at calculating the lengths of the fabulous material when people wanted to buy. 'Just smile,' Shiri instructed, 'and get Lavina to do that bit!' It was a wise decision. Some of the saris were decorated with gold and cost upwards of 60,000 rupees apiece. Initially, I was flabbergasted at how much people were prepared to spend on saris, especially when they were buying them en masse as part of a wedding trousseau.

I was polite, I worked hard as I had learnt to do (and as I liked doing), I was taught how to do good window displays. And I got on very well with the two sisters, who began to take me out and about with them to social gatherings. A few months after my arrival in Delhi they took me along to a party attended by all their rich, smart friends. As I had nothing appropriate to wear the sisters went through their collection of clothes and presented me with a beautiful grey sari embroidered with blue flowers. I loved it – I had never owned anything so gorgeous in my life. On the night of the party I stepped into my grey sari, my hair loose as I had yearned to wear it all my life, feeling like the aristocrat I was meant to be.

We approached the house through high wrought-iron gates and down a long drive. It was magnificent, with huge, solid wooden front doors under a white portico, beautiful tiled floors, and an army of white-uniformed servants. I was ushered into a vast room and found myself surrounded by a sea of sophistication. This was the Indian upper class, immaculately dressed, confident, understated, speaking English not in the usual sing-song Indian voice but in the crisp, clear tones of the BBC. To my surprise most of the women were smoking and drinking, activities I had never seen Indian women do before. This was the upper class and they clearly had different rules.

I stood there, trying not to gape, feeling rather self-conscious, aware that only a short time ago I had been a humble housemaid huddled under a thin blanket in a bare, unheated hotel room in Manali with my girlfriend, Dolma, trying to keep warm. I wondered if any of these Indian people could tell. To my surprise, I found myself surrounded by a group of guests who seemed eager to talk to me. They wanted to know all about Tibet, about my escape, about the Dalai Lama, and they listened in total silence as I quietly told them what I knew and what I had done. As well-informed, modern Indians they were intrigued by the recent appearance of Tibetans in the outside world and the rapidly growing popularity of Buddhism, particularly in the West. They had read many books about it, but I was the first 'real' Tibetan they had met.

One man was particularly pleasant. His name was Raunaq Yarkhan; he was single, with brown hair and very fair skin, and he was about 30 years old. He was charming, well-mannered and softly spoken, and I liked him immediately. Unlike most Indian men, who tried to touch my breast as they walked past me on the street, or pushed their bodies against mine on the buses, Raunaq was a complete gentleman. I felt I could relax with him and be myself. By the end of the evening he had told

In the plane on my flight to freedom.

On the beach at Brighton, in England, where I found my new home.

Outside my mother-in-law's house in Brighton.

Deckyi in her school in Mussorie.

me he had to go away on business and asked if I would like to house-sit for him. 'You will have the whole place to yourself, except for my servant,' he said. As I knew my living arrangement with Lavina was only meant to be temporary, I agreed. It was clear to me that his offer was genuine and in no way an attempt to take advantage of me, which proved to be true.

I found out later that Raunaq was the great-grandson of the famous Nizam of Hyderabad, once dubbed 'The Richest Man in the World'. The Nizam had been quite a character. His fortune was worth £500 million and included the Jacob Diamond, one of the biggest uncut diamonds in the world, which he used to use as a paperweight. Raunaq told me he had also been spectacularly mean. British visitors to his court were offered just one cup of tea, one biscuit and one cigarette. He would haggle over the price of a bag of sweets, and darn old clothes rather than buy new ones, even when he went to meet Nehru, India's first prime minister. He had so much money that he once hid £22 million in one of his palaces, and the rats ate it.

By the time Raunaq was born, the Nizam's palaces had become state property and his jewels were now kept in a bank vault. I never knew how much money Raunaq had, but he owned a lot of land in south India and had never really had to work in his life. In Tibet, my grandmother used to tell me stories about exotic kings and queens, princes and princesses from foreign lands, but I never dreamt I would actually meet one – let alone that someone like Raunaq would in time become a truly dear friend.

I moved into Raunaq's home in an exclusive part of Delhi to find myself surrounded by doctors, lawyers and diplomats, Mercedes and BMW cars. As soon as I walked through his door I thought, 'Wow – everything is so clean!' When you are poor it is immensely difficult to be clean. Without money there are no washing machines, sinks, hot water, showers, good quality soap or detergent. Penury means hovels, mud floors, tattered grubby clothes, old bedding, matted hair. It is almost impossible to look and keep clean. The dirt of poverty is utterly demoralising.

Raunaq's world, however, was gleaming. For the first time in my life I was given my own bedroom, with a high, comfortable double bed. It had a TV at the end which could receive all the channels. Now I could lie in bed and watch as much as I liked, without having to worry that the hotel management would catch me. I had a telephone, a state of the art bathroom.

I had gone from rags to riches – at least by association. From sleeping on the kitchen floor in Lhasa and living in a one-roomed hovel in Dharamsala, I was now surrounded by comfort. Karma is strange, I thought, you never know which way it is going to swing. The Buddha said it all depends on which of the many seeds you are carrying is going to ripen.

Completing my total reversal of fortune, I now had a servant to do all the cleaning, housework and washing. He even cooked my meals. It was surreal. I have to say, this part of the deal made me extremely uncomfortable. I didn't like anyone cleaning up after me and doing my washing! After decades of being everyone else's servant it seemed completely wrong. I constantly tried to help him, but he would be offended. 'No, I need to do this myself,' he insisted. 'If I don't I will get bored and I may also get the sack.' At least he let me wash my own underwear.

My house-sitting duties were minimal. I was only required to keep an eye on things when Raunaq was away, and take telephone messages, so I kept up my job at the sari shop. I always felt happier when I was working.

Somehow the house-sitting arrangement became permanent. When Raunaq was in town we got on extremely well, living together like brother and sister. He was a quiet man who liked to read the papers every morning. I never saw him lift a finger around the house – he wasn't able even to make toast or boil himself a cup of tea because he had always had servants to do it. But he was very kind, driving me to work if I was running late, and frequently including me in his social life.

And so I was delighted but certainly not fazed when I was invited to spend a week with his family in Hyderabad, due south of Delhi. I spent two glorious days alone on a train getting there, looking through the train window at the fascinating sights and the beautiful Indian countryside. I suspected that the family wanted to check me out in case I was trying to ensnare Raunaq as a husband, but they need not have worried. Our relationship was totally platonic and Raunaq seemed as uninterested as I was in getting married. It is hard for upper-class Indians to find suitable wives.

A servant picked me up at the station and whisked me into a world of elegance. The family home was no longer a palace, but it was large and surrounded by well-manicured lawns, flowerbeds, and an orchard. There were countless bedrooms, and a sumptuous dining room with cabinets filled with antique glasses, silver cutlery and fine bone-china dinner services. Raunaq's father was dead but I met his mother, a tall, charming woman who welcomed me graciously. She was beautifully dressed and had the same fair skin as Raunaq. When I asked her about it she told me they had Russian blood in their veins. Raunaq's sister, a doctor in New York, was there too and together they showed me the family album of their relatives at the height of their power. Looking at the Nizam's picture, I noticed he had a round face, downward-sloping eyes and thin, sensitive fingers, and was decked out in masses of jewels. The family palace had been huge – but not, I noted, as big as the Potala.

Raunaq's family were extremely hospitable. They took me around Hyderabad to show me the schools, the hospitals and the university the Nizam had built for his subjects. He was clearly a caring man as well as a very rich one. Every morning I was sent a fresh coconut to drink from before going down for breakfast, which was a spread of Indian and Western dishes.

Everything was very formal, which was not my style at all. What I found particularly strange, and a little arduous, was that all the meals were served at precisely the same time every day – including morning coffee and afternoon tea, when little cakes and pancakes were offered. Tibetans are never time-bound like this. We prefer to be free, not bound by the clock – which means we are often late! If you wanted a simple cup of tea between meals in this household, it took at least two hours to reach you. 'What's wrong?' I asked Raunaq on one such occasion. 'Well, the first servant tells the second servant, and so on down the line until the message gets to the tea maker,' he said. Being rich clearly didn't make life any easier!

Personally I had no desire to emulate Raunaq or his family, and had never harboured any ambition to be wealthy myself. What I did appreciate, however, was the opportunity to see how high society and wealthy people lived. I always wanted to learn, to broaden my horizons.

Raunaq's friends were also very charming, pleasant people, and not at all snobby. They treated me like one of their own. I got on particularly well with Arun Khanna, a descendant of the Maharajah of Patiala, who had been poisoned by the British. He told me his ancestor had had 300 concubines. I was absolutely fascinated. How could any man cope with that many women, I wondered.

Arun was a joker with a long moustache waxed at the ends like his great-grandfather. One day he invited me for a swim in his pool. 'No Tibetan swims. I don't know how,' I said in alarm. 'No problem, I'll teach you,' he replied. I am game for almost anything, but getting into a costume and baring my body to that extent did not feel at all right. I gave it a go, but nearly drowned. 'I'm a mountain woman, not a sea woman!' I shouted.

More usefully, my new friends began to teach me how to behave in contemporary, sophisticated society. They showed me how to eat with a knife and fork, implements I had seen before only on TV. Until then I had only eaten soup, noodles and dumplings out of a bowl, with a spoon and chopsticks. Now I discovered tablecloths and napkins. And they showed me what was expected in their world. 'When you meet people you must stand up straight, look them in the eye, and shake them by the hand,' they instructed.

This was completely contrary to upper-class Tibetan social mores, where you are meant to keep your head bowed, your hands together and your eyes lowered to the floor as a sign of politeness. In my country the more humble and modest you appear, the higher bred you are considered to be. 'You don't have to grovel. You can be confident and proud of yourself,' these Indian women wearing jeans told me. They also showed me it was perfectly ladylike to cross my legs, a habit considered exceedingly rude and inappropriate in Tibet. I was eager and willing to learn the ways of the world as quickly as I could.

Some modern customs, however, I thought I could leave well alone. One man I met decided his nose was too big (although it looked fine to me) and he paid an enormous sum of money to have it altered by plastic surgery. Afterwards it looked exactly the same and I couldn't understand why he didn't ask for his money back. If you have money you can do anything you want, even stupid things, I thought sadly. If I had had even a little more money I would have been able to support Deckyi and would never have had to let her go.

On the face of it my life had improved beyond measure. I had kind, rich, interesting friends. I had a job. I had a comfortable place to stay and I was earning money. Not far beneath the surface, however, was a gnawing pain and guilt over Deckyi. True to their word, her grandparents had kept a blanket silence over her whereabouts and well-being. Nevertheless, I thought about her constantly and missed her terribly. Whenever I talked about her the tears would flow – I cried a lot in the shop with Lavina and Shiri when there were no customers about. Her photograph was still on my altar next to the Buddha, and I still offered her sweets.

After two years in Delhi I made the journey back to Dharamsala to see if her grandparents had brought her back, as they had said they would. But I couldn't find her anywhere and no one had heard anything of her. On my return to Delhi, desperate for news, I decided to try and get in touch with her father, Tenzin. Surely he would know what had happened to his daughter. I went to Tibet House and asked them to contact their New York office, as I was trying to get in touch with the man with whom I had had a child. Sure enough, a few weeks later a letter arrived from Tibet House in New York giving Tenzin's address and telephone number.

It cost a lot of money to call the USA but I did not care. Tentatively, I dialled. I heard the phone ringing and a man's voice answered. It was Tenzin. 'It's me, Soname,' I said. 'Please, let me speak. I'm not calling because I want anything from you. I don't want money, I don't want to interfere with your life at all, but I'm desperate to know what has happened to Deckyi. I haven't heard from her for two years and this is very difficult for me. Is she all right? Is she getting an education? Where is she?'

There was complete silence at the other end. He did not say a single word. I kept talking, begging him for information, but still he did not speak. I was devastated. How could he do this to me? Our relationship may have been over but we had gone through a lot together. We had shared a child! What had this man become? Sobbing now, I said into the mouthpiece, 'You have changed too much.' His refusal to talk to me was cruel. I wondered if money or his career had corrupted him.

I had hit a wall. As far as Deckyi was concerned, whichever way I turned I could not win. Even if I knew where she was I still would not be able to look after her. There was nowhere for her to live, and my salary wouldn't stretch to food for two, let alone a rented flat. I finally had the freedom and independence that I yearned for, and which I had risked my life in order to find, and yet I was not free at all. My heart was tied to a little girl who ruled me. The only thing I could do was to keep my mind positive and survive myself. I fervently believed that if I could stay strong my daughter would stay strong too. There is an unbreakable link between mother and child, and I knew whatever happened to me would affect her, through thought waves or some other invisible pathway. And I lived in hope that one day I would find Deckyi again and be reunited with her. It was the best, indeed the only, way I could think of to help my daughter.

And so I got on with my life, filling it with work, social activities and music. My inherent love of music had not diminished. I sang all the time when I was alone, and listened to different types of music on the radio. It was in Delhi that I first heard world music, and I was drawn to it immediately. This is my kind of sound, I thought, this is where my voice fits. In Delhi I also began to meet Westerners for the first time, introduced by Raunaq, Shiri and their friends. I loved speaking to them to practise my English, which I was keen to master. I had been in the capital long enough by now to know that without English you could get nowhere in today's world. If I could not get an education at school or university, then English was the next best thing. I already knew Hindi, as well as Chinese and Tibetan, and English would be the jewel in the crown.

At every opportunity I sat down in cafés and chatted to Westerners. My initial impression was that Westerners, especially the men, were all very mild and gentle, both in their manner and their speech. It was a surprise. Westerners' bodies may be big, strong and hairy, I thought, but inside they are soft and sensitive. Maybe it was because they had easy, comfortable lives and didn't have to fight for survival like most Asian people. When you are locked in a daily battle for food and shelter, to feed your children, and you suffer years of persecution like the Tibetans, you toughen up inside.

One day a Kashmiri friend introduced me to Marc, a Frenchman who was to be pivotal in shaping the next stage of my life. Marc was young, blond, blue eyed, and exceptionally handsome like a model. Broken-hearted over a failed love affair, he was also broke financially. He was in a bad way and I took pity on him. I lent him money, and took him out to dinner to try and cheer him up. 'Forget it, there will be another girl for you who you will love as much,' I told him. But he was hard to shift and kept crying.

After that Marc used to visit my home frequently. One evening he turned to me and said: 'Why don't you come to France?' The idea appealed instantly to my adventurous spirit. 'Why not! Thank you!' I replied. 'I would love to see Europe and all those famous places like Paris and London. It will help with my education.' I thought I would go away for a year, or 18 months at most, and then come back to India. It seemed a great idea. I would go to France and then move on to England where I knew another man, Michael Windsor, whom I had also met in Delhi. Michael was an older man whom I had bumped into – literally – in a café in Delhi. He was coming out as I was going in and we collided in the doorway. He smiled, I smiled back, and then he was gone. About an hour later I was walking home when he came out of a hotel and bumped into me again. We looked at each other in surprise. 'Are you Japanese?' he asked. I don't know why so many people think I'm Japanese – but we began to talk. He said he was on his way to buy a motorbike to ship back to England and wondered if I would mind coming with him to translate for him from Hindi. I had nothing else to do and Michael seemed like a nice man, so in keeping with my trusting nature I agreed. We hopped into a rickshaw together, and I helped him buy the bike. Afterwards he said, 'I'm going back to England late tonight, but will you have a meal with me before I go?' And so I went to dinner with him. I had a pleasant time and we swapped addresses.

After visiting Michael, then, maybe, I could see the rest of Europe. There was nothing to keep me in Delhi. I still had no relationship (I loved Marc very much, but like a brother). I had no career. I was working extremely hard but my salary was only enough to keep me in the Indian capital and I had no prospects. I could see no way of rising beyond working in a sari shop. Having lost contact with Deckyi completely, I did not think it made any difference whether I was in India or France.

The West glittered like the golden roofs of the Potala. There has to be more to life than this, I mused. I am sure I can do better for myself. I wanted my life to amount to something. It was the same drive that had urged me to escape in the first place.

But first I had to get travel documents and British and French visas. It took time, hours of tedious form filling and endless waiting in government queues, but eventually I was given a one-year French student visa and a Yellow Travel Document – not exactly a passport, but a certificate designed for refugees to allow them to enter and leave foreign countries. For the first time in my life I felt almost legal.

While I was waiting for my papers to come through, Marc returned to France, where he would wait for me. Before he left he took me to Delhi airport to show me the intricacies of aeroplane travel. He pointed out the check-in desks and the departure boards, telling me to ask the check-in girl very clearly for my flight number and to make sure every few steps that I was heading for the right departure gate. I memorised it all extremely carefully, hoping I could do it.

After his departure I wrote Marc a letter: 'You have given me the opportunity of a new life. Thank you. I promise I will not waste it.' But now that France looked a real possibility rather than merely a good idea, I began to feel nervous. After all, this was the West. The rich West where if you worked hard you could change your life for ever. The decadent West where women displayed their bodies, where everyone got drunk, took drugs, and changed sexual partners regularly. The frantic, rushing, clockbound West, where no one had time to stop in the street for a chat even with their friends. The clever, intelligent West, where the whole of life was run by computers.

This notion in particular petrified me. I had no idea how to work a computer. How would I ever find a job? What would I do? At least I can try and learn French, I thought. I loved the sound of the language and couldn't wait to speak it. Consequently, I enrolled in a French language school and every morning for six months before I went to work I tried to get my tongue around the strange, beautiful sounds. As usual, my attempts at formal learning were an abysmal failure. I was the only Tibetan in a class of 60 and I spent much of my time chatting away in Hindi. It was fun, but I learnt nothing.

I now had my travel documents but I was so apprehensive that I delayed buying a plane ticket. I may have been bold, may have led a gypsy life since leaving Tibet, but getting on a plane and going to Europe was like flying to the moon. It was daunting. But finally, two days before my French visa was due to expire, I leapt. In October 1997, Raunaq's driver took me to the airport. No one came to see me off, but no one ever has. Raunaq had given me over 3,000 rupees (the equivalent of £400), wished me well, and told me that if France did not work out there would always be a home waiting for me in Delhi. Wearing a turquoise *chuba* and clutching a dilapidated suitcase tied up with rope, I boarded an Aeroflot flight – the cheapest I could find – bound for Paris. How could I have ever imagined when I escaped from Tibet, nine years previously, that my flight to freedom would take me this far?

CHAPTER TWELVE

The West

A S THE PLANE left the dry, scorched earth of India and soared into the bright blue sky, my fear evaporated and was replaced with a tingling excitement. I was flying!

For a poor Tibetan country girl to be on a plane going anywhere, let alone the West, was an incredible achievement. Nobody from Yarlung had ever been on a plane. In fact, nobody in the whole of Tibet had even seen a plane until as late as the mid-1980s when tourists began jetting in to Lhasa. Then the sight of an enormous 'iron bird', as we called it, descending from the sky seemed to us literally like a visitation of beings from another planet. The Tibetans had always believed in other galaxies peopled by different life forms, and so such an event was highly plausible to us. All the traffic in Lhasa would come to a halt and everybody would stop what they were doing to watch in awe and amazement.

Now I myself was inside an iron bird, flying through the sky, feeling wonderful. Who would have believed it? If only my family could see me now, I thought. But of course my family had no idea where I was, let alone what I was doing.

The plane turned north. I looked down from my window seat and there at 26,000 feet, appearing so close I thought I could touch them, were the magnificent, rugged, snow-capped Himalayas. They were like a massive, solid wall separating my country from the rest of the world. I gasped. They were a breathtaking sight, and higher than I had ever imagined. My eagle-eye view finally gave me a true sense of what I had had to climb to gain my freedom. No wonder I had nearly died of exhaustion.

I sat back and began to enjoy myself. Up there, on my own, flying above the clouds I was in my element – unbounded, weightless, free. It was rather like being in the Bardo, I surmised, having left one life behind and not having yet arrived in the next. There was a sense of spaciousness in that state.

My fellow passengers were a jolly lot – a mixture of Indian, Pakistani and Russian workers. Soon the vodka started to flow and they began to sing. It was like a festival. Everything about that flight was spell-binding, including the lunch served in tiny portions on a tray, like baby food. It was delicious. I don't know why my friends had shaken their heads in horror when I told them I was flying Aeroflot.

My adventure continued at Moscow airport where I had to change planes. I couldn't understand a word anyone said, nor recognise any of the strange writing. I resorted to shouting 'Paris, Paris,' at various people and waving my boarding pass at them. Miraculously I was steered to the right departure gate and somehow managed to catch the connection.

The flight to France was short but the wait at Immigration was horribly long. I held my breath as a baffled immigration officer inspected my Tibetan Refugee Yellow Travel Document. After many questions and phone calls to his superiors, he finally gave me a 90-day stamp and let me into France.

My battered old suitcase was waiting for me, but Marc wasn't. There was no sign of him anywhere. I sat down to wait, watching while my fellow passengers were greeted and then all left. I began to feel a little anxious. Had I been abandoned in a totally strange country, not knowing where to go or how things worked? I walked around the airport for a while but after three hours Marc still had not showed up. I decided I would sleep rough on one of the airport benches. Things would work themselves out in the morning, I thought optimistically.

Suddenly Marc came bursting through the doors, in a terrible panic. He had gone to the wrong Paris airport. I hugged him, really happy to see my old friend again. He put me in his little car and whisked me off to Tours, where he lived in a ground-floor flat in a big house. I never stopped talking from the moment he picked me up, regaling him with the details of my journey. I was so excited. 'I've thought and talked about the West for a year and now I'm actually here,' I said.

The next morning I woke, still swaying from jet lag, but determined to start exploring. Our first stop was a hypermarket. It looked like a government building to me; never had I seen a shop so large. The doors opened by themselves. 'Where's the doorman?' I asked. 'There isn't one. The doors open electronically,' Marc replied. This was magic. Intrigued, I kept walking in and out.

Once inside I took one look at the sheer scale of the store, the shelves groaning with unfamiliar products, and declared, 'You can leave me here. Come back in two hours.' I knew exactly where I was heading first – the toiletry section. I had been in love with Western soaps, shampoos and body lotions ever since I had smelt the first tourists who came to Lhasa. We had nothing as good in Tibet or India and I longed to own some. I undid lots of tops and smelt them all. Then I spied people moving up a staircase without walking. Fascinated, I thought I would give it a try. I got on the moving stairs all right but when I got to the top I was thrown on to the floor. I landed flat on my face, my hair sprawled in front of me like a carpet and the contents of my shopping basket scattered everywhere. People came running from all directions to see if I was hurt. But my body was OK, it was only my pride that was dented. I watched for a long time before daring to go down, studying how people put one foot out when they reached the bottom. I copied and took a great leap. I looked ridiculous, but at least I was safe.

Over the next few weeks, when he was not at work, Marc drove me around showing me the sights of this new world. My first, overriding impression of the West was how extraordinarily clean, well-kept, comfortable and affluent it was. The streets did not smell of urine and faeces as they did in Delhi, the roads had no potholes. Trees had even been planted along their edges to make them more attractive. I went to the zoo and saw the animals given meat that people in Tibet and India would never be able to afford – and they had toys and small houses in their cages. There was even a little train to take us around the zoo if we were tired. In France the electricity never went on and off as it did in India and there was hot water day and night, whenever you wanted it. I did not understand how people could be making the electricity 24 hours a day. The post always arrived, and nothing had been stolen from it.

Life was exceedingly easy in the West, but there was much that was strange. The first time I went to visit Marc's parents for dinner I tucked into the delicious bread that was served with the soup because I was hungry, not realising there were two more courses to follow. When she brought them out I couldn't eat them, I was too full. I was very embarrassed. 'Why didn't your mother put all the dishes on the table at once, like we do? She's making a lot of unnecessary work for herself going in and out of the kitchen all the time, changing the cutlery and the plates,' I remarked later to Marc.

Bringing flowers for someone was another new custom. We never pick flowers in Tibet, believing they should be left to bloom for the whole of their natural life to give pleasure to many people, rather than dying after three days. When we go to someone's house we take eggs or biscuits.

I loved the French countryside. I roamed the fields, picking wild strawberries, getting to know the farming people who allowed me to eat the cherry tomatoes and fruit they were harvesting. Marc's sister had a beautiful house with plenty of land, a vegetable garden and two horses. I used to lie on her lawn looking up the sky, drinking in the smell of the earth and the freshness of the air. After Delhi it was balm to my soul. I was back in the midst of nature, where I always felt most at home.

In France, I began to experience another type of freedom – freedom as a woman. It was a new sensation that made me heady with joy. In Asia, no matter how educated a woman is, she is always confined by society's rules. She has to watch herself constantly and simply cannot say and do as she wishes. In India, for example, I couldn't talk to beggars without being thought of as low status myself. In Dharamsala I couldn't have dinner with a man alone without being called a prostitute. If you are pretty and dress nicely, as Dolma and I used to do in Manali, you are called easy girls. I found it painfully constricting, living amid such petty-mindedness and gossip.

In the East, image and 'face' is all-important. How you present yourself in public is how you are judged. A lot of judging goes on in the East. Where is the freedom in that? To my mind these rules were not only absurd but were not a spiritual way of thinking. I wanted to talk to anybody I wished, and not have to worry all the time about my appearance. In France, I began to see that no one cared what I was wearing or how I behaved on account of my sex. I don't think Western women realise how unbelievably fortunate they are, how rare their situation is.

In celebration of my new-found liberty I decided to cut off my hair. It had never been cut in all my 24 years, and it reached down to my calves. People would turn their heads to look at me. I wanted to blend in, to look more like the elegant, modern, chic French women I saw. It was time to chop off my hair and step into the contemporary Western world. I wanted a brand new image to fit my new start in life.

'Are you sure?' asked Marc, when I told him. 'Perfectly,' I replied. 'In that case I'll take you to the best hairdresser in town,' he replied, entering into the spirit of things.

The hairdresser balked a little when I indicated what I wanted but she began to chop. After some hours I emerged with my hair cropped close to my head and shaped into a 'V' at the back. I loved it! Walking along the pavement, it felt as though the great weight of my past had been lifted from me.

To complete my transformation Marc took me to Paris to buy trousers and shirts, Western outfits to complete my metamorphosis. Paris was beautiful, but I was surprised to see black people and Asians there. 'Wow, so the West isn't all white!' I said to Marc. Finally, I was being educated. I had to see the great Christian cathedrals too and so we went to Sacre Coeur and Notre-Dame. I found them magnificent, but rather empty, not dark, cosy and intimate like the Jokhang.

I had been in France about a month when I realised it wasn't possible for me to stay. I loved it there and felt very happy, but I was running out of money and had to get a job. Marc had been wonderfully hospitable, but I did not want to lean on him for much longer. He tried to get me work looking after a blind man, but the language was a problem. I decided to move on to England, to see London and broaden my horizons further. I wrote to the one English person I knew, Michael Windsor, telling him I was in France. 'Come and visit, bring Marc too,' he replied.

Michael lived in Brighton, on the south coast, by the sea, and Marc insisted on coming with me to check him out. We drove all the way to England, taking in Amsterdam and Belgium en route. Getting the ferry was another new experience. I had seen large bodies of water before as there were huge lakes in Tibet, but I had never been on a boat. Stepping on board, I could not believe it had a casino, cinema, disco, swimming pool, restaurants, bars, and a huge car park where everyone put their vehicles. As soon as the boat began to sway I got seasick – but even that didn't quell my excitement.

When we docked in England I had the usual problems with the immigration officers. They questioned me for hours, in spite of the fact I had a valid British visa. Thankfully Marc fielded all their queries, assuring them he would take responsibility for me, and only then did they let us pass. I would have been completely lost without Marc, and I was very grateful. By the time we were released and finally got into our car, it was late. I was exhausted,

I didn't feel very well, and I immediately fell asleep.

I woke up to find Marc shaking me. 'We're here,' he said. I looked out of the window to see an ornate, domed building. 'Is England a Muslim country?' I asked. Marc laughed. 'No, that's the Brighton Pavilion,' he replied.

Michael came to meet us and took us back to his house, where he made us comfortable. The following day, announcing that it was 'a typical English dish', he took us out for fish and chips. Like most Tibetans I don't like fish very much, so I asked if there was anything else on the menu. 'No, this is all they serve,' he said. I thought that very strange. 'Is this the only food you have in Britain?' I enquired anxiously. 'No, we have other food, including Indian and Chinese,' he replied. I was relieved to hear that. Maybe I won't die of starvation here after all, I thought.

After a week Marc returned to France. 'This Michael is a nice man,' he said, 'you'll be OK with him.' When he turned to go I had tears in my eyes. I was very fond of Marc. He had been so kind to me, and he had shared my very first days in the West.

It was November when I arrived in Brighton and the weather was turning cold, ready for winter. It began to get dark early in the afternoon and most of the time there was a steady drizzle in a grey sky. I loved it! I revelled in the moist, cool air that wrapped itself around my face and hair. In this temperature I could breathe. Here there were no mosquitoes. The English climate is definitely for me, I decided.

Not everything in this new land was so pleasing, however. I was not very keen on the pubs that Michael took me to. I only ever drank tea and lemonade, and I hated the smoky atmosphere, and people getting drunk. But Michael seemed to enjoy them, so I continued to go with him. After a while, though, my independent streak came out and I said I preferred to stay at home. Michael's house was frankly a mess. There was dust everywhere, there were old dishes in the sink, and his oven didn't look as if anyone had ever been near it. It was thick with grease. With my innate love of order and cleanliness, I simply could not stand it. For three days I scrubbed, cleaned, swept and dusted. And I began to feel quite settled.

Michael was tall, honest and good looking – and 20 years older than me. By trade he was a self-employed carpet-fitter, but he also had a business importing Indian furniture. He spent a lot of time in India, a country he adored. He was a good man. We got on well, I enjoyed being with him and, most important, he made me laugh. We began to have a lot of fun together. He was highly individualistic and very much his own person – like me. With Michael I found I could be myself. Within a few short weeks, much to my surprise, I had fallen in love.

It was not what I had expected, nor what I had in mind when I came to England. Romance was the last thing I was looking for. My experience with men had hardly been successful; I was badly scarred and had steered clear of romantic liaisons for years. But Michael was different. He was kind and gentle (as all Western men still seemed to me) and never tried to get into bed with me. I appreciated that. With Michael I felt safe, and this time my feelings were reciprocated. When Christmas came, my first Christmas in England, he gave me five presents. Overcome, I promptly burst into tears. No one had ever given me a present before.

Two months later he asked me to marry him and without hesitation I said yes. It just seemed right. Like all my life-changing decisions I acted spontaneously, from the heart, trusting my intuition. My intended one-year visit to the West had suddenly, dramatically, turned into something much more long term. By agreeing to marry Michael I realised I was turning my back on my roots, my past and all that was familiar, committing myself to starting afresh and living in a foreign land, amid strangers with an alien culture. But in him I saw a good man whom I loved and who loved me. With Michael I felt I could have a future.

I certainly wasn't marrying him for his money, because he was not well off. But I believed I could have a settled life with him, could find work myself and build up some money of my own. And then, one day, when I found Deckyi, I would have something truly solid and wonderful to offer her – a home, enough food and lots of emotional security. I would make up for all the years of separation and for my madness at letting her go. And then we could be close again, like a mother and daughter ought to be. That was my dream. Marrying Michael was wonderfully worthwhile.

Early one summer morning in 1998, I put on my turquoise *chuba* and went to the Brighton register office to get married. A few days previously Michael had fallen off his motorbike and broken his ankle, and he cut a splendid figure as he hobbled up on crutches. I said my vows in halting English, and emerged an officially married woman for the first time. I was blissfully happy. We will be together for the rest of our lives, I vowed, I shall be a good wife and do my very best to make Michael happy.

Our reception was held in a pub. Loads of Michael's friends and family came, but there was no one there for me. It made me sad – on this particular day I missed my family, and especially my mother, very much. But Michael's mother was extremely warm and welcoming, and I learnt to call her 'Mother' as she requested (although it didn't feel the same as saying it to my true mother). Over time I grew to love her very much, and she in turn cared for me like a daughter, confiding in me about her life, holding my hand when we walked down the street together, never siding with either Michael or me if we had had an argument.

Every Sunday we went to her house for a traditional roast lunch, after which I would wash up. I love roast meat – we never cooked meat in ovens in Tibet. Michael's father had died four years before I came to England, which was a great pity as I heard he was a marvellous man. There was a brother too, who I got on extremely well with. Being part of a family again was wonderful, deeply healing. It had been twenty years since I had last experienced anything like it, when I was a very little girl in Yarlung, surrounded by the warmth of my parents, grandparents, siblings, aunts, uncles and cousins. 'You should never take your family for granted because you don't realise how precious they are. Go and see them as often as possible, while you still have them.' That was what I told Michael, all his friends and anyone who would listen.

I was very content with Michael. In a short time he became everything to me: father, brother, mother and husband all rolled into one. I gave him all my love. We told each other everything. Somehow, being married, and feeling emotionally secure, released decades of pain and trauma that had been locked up inside me. I would snuggle up next to him and tell him about the years when I was a child slave, wrenched from my mother, deprived of warmth and affection, ruled by a regime of relentless strict discipline. I told him of my aching loneliness and how surviving had made me strong. I told him how I had watched my mother die and how cold everything had seemed afterwards. And I told him about Deckyi, my anguish at losing her and my constant worry not knowing where she was or what she was doing.

As I spoke the tears poured down. I cried for the loss of it all – my country, my childhood, my mother, my education, my daughter. And I wept for my own bravery and how I had been prepared to risk my life in order to find freedom.

For many nights I cried into Michael's shoulder and he would put his arms around me and comfort me. As the feelings came tumbling out, I regressed to babyhood. Me, who had been the pillar of self-sufficiency and strength all my life! I went out and bought a baby's bottle. I would fill it with milk and go to sleep at night sucking it. It did not bother Michael at all. 'If that's what you need to do, go ahead,' he said. After a few weeks, that deprived child had been comforted and I didn't need to do it any more. I threw the bottle away and never picked one up again.

During the day, however, I became my usual independent self once more. I loved Michael, but that did not mean I was obsessed. I might be married but I was still a free spirit. We agreed that we would allow each other the freedom to be ourselves, and not live in each other's pockets. It worked well: being married to someone from a different culture could be tricky at times, as we had such contrasting attitudes to life. He liked going to the pub and socialising, I preferred staying at home, being quiet and watching TV. He liked English food, I liked Asian, and so we cooked our own meals. We also liked eating at different times. I didn't like playing card games or chess, although I did try my hand at golf.

But we both enjoyed going for walks in the country. I found the English green unimaginably beautiful. Nepal is lush and exotic, but nothing compares to the bright emerald green of the English countryside or the radiant brightness of the spring flowers and blossoms. I loved looking at the cows and sheep, because they reminded me a little of Tibet. But the farms puzzled me. In Tibet you always saw the farmer and his helpers ploughing or herding, but I never saw anyone working in the English fields. These farms seemed to look after themselves.

My fiercely independent, proud nature meant I didn't want to lean on Michael financially. I had always worked and now I quickly got a job, looking after an old lady, the mother of one of Michael's friends, for two afternoons a week. It wasn't much, but it was a start. About 85 years old, she had once been a synchronised swimmer but now she could hardly walk. She broke my heart. She lived all alone and her son only visited her for ten minutes at a time. She was unbearably lonely. In Tibet we never leave elderly mothers to live by themselves – a family member always stays at home to look after them.

I tried to treat this old lady like my own mother. I cut her toenails, bought cream from the chemist to put on her feet and soaked them in hot water. I curled her hair and put make-up on her face, showing her in the mirror. I made her wear warmer clothes because she was often cold. She hardly ate, but would do so if I ate with her. I fed her like a baby. And I would sit and listen for hours while she told me all about her past, staying much longer than I was paid for. 'You didn't come and see me yesterday or the day before,' she used to say, and so I would go more often, always without pay.

I felt compassion for her. Soon she began to trust me and would ask me to take money out of her purse to buy cigarettes and biscuits. When she died, three months later, I went to her funeral. I liked the service but I was deeply shocked when afterwards everyone went to the pub and had a party. In Tibet, if a family member dies, we grieve for a year. We don't wash our face or our hair for a month (some people go mad with grief), and we certainly don't play music, or have fun. I felt like saying 'You've got no respect,' but I realised I was in a different culture and there was nothing I could say.

I now needed to find other work. Cleaning was what I knew best and so I took jobs first washing up at the Masonic lodge and later, cleaning at the police station. The latter was a bit of a joke. Legally I was not supposed to earn my living at all, even though I had married an Englishman. My old terrible karma with legal status had resurfaced once more. With no official papers it had been impossible for me to live in my own country, and now it was happening again in England.

Michael and I had gone to a solicitor before we married to ask advice about my residency, but she had said there was no hurry as I still had some months left on my visa. When we finally did fill out all the forms she told us we should have done it before we got married. So we went to a second solicitor, who told us it didn't matter. And so the muddle went on. These solicitors had studied the same law but they all had different opinions about it – it was all rather like India, I thought.

Finally Michael submitted an account of his earnings and the forms were sent to the Home Office. We were told we would have to wait two years for my papers to be processed. During this time, I was informed, I could not leave the country, not even for day trip, nor could I work. I was meant to sit around doing nothing and contributing nothing to the country. It was crazy!

Michael and I found it pretty stressful dealing with the officialdom and the uncertainty. We couldn't even go on holiday to France together to see Marc. Being without an identity is a horrible feeling, like being a ghost. To all intents and purposes you don't exist – officially, at least.

Never being one to sit around, as I had been ordered to do, I continued to work at my part-time jobs. For five years I stacked the dishwasher and scrubbed pots at the Masonic lodge, growing big arm muscles as I did so. I was paid £3.75 an hour, £60 a week. My employers said I was the best worker they had ever had. 'We'll tell the Dalai Lama how great you are!' they joked. Every Christmas they gave me a present. They were astonished how strong I was – and at my ability to lift several full black rubbish-bin liners at once. 'You should have seen me carrying wet carpets as a kid in Lhasa,' I retorted.

Washing up was exhausting, especially because I again worked far longer hours than I was paid for. I could not stand not doing a job properly, so I felt compelled to finish the work that others had left. Eventually I moved on to the police station, where the work was infinitely lighter – dusting, vacuuming and tidying the offices – and I worked just four hours a day, from 6 am to 10 am or from 4 pm to 8 pm.

Whatever my work schedule, though, every day I woke up at 4 am to say my prayers and perform my meditation, as I had done since I lived with the Dalai Lama in Dharamsala. I prayed for the end of suffering for all sentient beings. I visualised my family, my friends, my enemies and as many faceless strangers as I could sitting around me, and 'saw' the Buddha emanating streams of healing golden light, filling us all with love, compassion and wisdom. And right in front of me I visualised Deckyi, my daughter, and prayed from the bottom of my heart that she was safe and well, and that we would be together again one day.

CHAPTER THIRTEEN

Finding My Voice

APART FROM THE PERPETUAL ACHE of missing my daughter, I was settling well into Western life, getting used to the English way of doing things. A few months into married life I experienced my first church wedding; that of two of Michael's friends. It was a glorious day. The Christian ceremony was fascinating and the bride looked beautiful dressed all in white. When it was over we walked from the church to the reception. There was much laughter, food and drink, but to my dismay, no singing. How could you have a wedding celebration without singing! In Tibet no marriage takes place without music.

'Shall I sing you a Tibetan song to bless the couple?' I tentatively asked. I had never been shy of singing. The guests looked a little surprised but then said, 'Come on.' Boldly I stood up and, without a microphone, sang one of my childhood songs. There was silence, then thunderous applause. 'Sing another one!' they all shouted. I sang them another, and another.

Afterwards, when the fuss had died down, a man approached me, introducing himself as a former member of the famous punk group, The Sex Pistols. 'I'm going to Germany touring with my own group. Will you join us? I'll pay all your expenses. I love your voice,' he said. I was dumbfounded – and thrilled. I never thought my voice was anything special. Sadly, there was no way I could take up his offer because legally I was not allowed to leave Britain. If I did, I would never be able to get back in again. Letting this golden opportunity go was a blow – but the fact that someone had thought I was good enough to sing professionally, together with all the praise I had received at the wedding, boosted my confidence tremendously. Maybe I could earn my living using my voice.

As though this was exactly the right course of action, from then on life began to present me with opportunities to sing. Not long after the wedding I met a musician in Brighton named Geoff Smith. A well-known professional dulcimer player who had designed his own instrument with 160 strings, he had heard of me via friends and was interested in teaming up, as he was fascinated by Eastern tunings. All my life I had always sung solo – either in front of my family in Yarlung as a child, or in Lhasa when the Tashis used to make me sing for their guests at New Year while they downed their liquor. (I remember everyone laughing at me, a little girl singing the Chinese love songs I had picked up from the tape recorder.) Now I had to learn to sing accompanied by another musician.

It required listening to Geoff, being mindful of his playing – and being patient. I couldn't just open my mouth and sing when I felt like it. But with a little practice I soon got the hang of it. I had always had a good ear, and since my Delhi days had listened avidly to all types of world music. Since coming to England I had become a great fan of Bulgarian music in particular.

When Geoff thought we were ready he suggested we perform together during the Brighton Festival. This would be my first professional appearance and I was terribly nervous. It was one thing to sing spontaneously at a wedding, but another to stand up on a stage and sing to a paying audience.

In my culture such a thing is unheard of. No one in Tibet sings for money. Singing is part of our culture, not a job. We sing when we are building houses; we sing when we plough the fields; we sing when the yak is getting bored. We tap out tunes on pieces of wood, or on the *damyang*, the Tibetan guitar. Sometimes we even sing snatches of Tibetan opera. I remember how, during the summer months, people would go camping. The women would bring their laundry from home and wash it in the river, the men would play games, the children would dash about, and everybody would be singing and dancing. So, to put myself up as 'a singer' in front of rows of people was anathema. 'What on earth am I doing?' I said to myself, as I prepared to perform my first gig. My father's words came winging back: 'Anyone who publicly stands up and sings is worse than a performing monkey.' Being a singer was definitely not respectable for a Tibetan woman of my background.

I sang without a mike, Geoff accompanying me. It was scary and exhilarating at the same time. When it was over I looked at the audience and several people were crying. And we went on from there. Our next gig was at Borders Bookshop in Brighton for the launch of a photographic book on Tibet. Again crowds gathered to listen.

Soon my singing career began to take off. Two months later I was asked, along with a number of other musicians, to perform at The End nightclub, in London, to celebrate Tibetan New Year. The BBC picked up the event and asked me to do an interview and a song for a programme called *Outlook*, which was broadcast all around the world. I had to sing for four minutes precisely – another new discipline to master. I wondered if anyone I knew in India or even Tibet had heard me.

Several other BBC radio programmes, including *Woman's Hour*, now contacted me, fascinated by my story and my voice. They told me they had received an exceptionally large response from their listeners. A man called Byron Allen was moved enough to write a poem which the producer forwarded on to me. It ended:

> Sounds are swooping away in all directions,
> Only the fading, breathy, single, simple

Note
Dying into silence
Then a woman yearning in a language you don't understand
But yearning.

At first I sang the traditional songs I had been taught at my grandmother's knee, but gradually a new spirit of creativity that I did not know I possessed began to take hold and I began to think up my own compositions. Funnily enough, I gained quite a lot of inspiration while I was working at the Masonic lodge washing up. As I scoured the big cooking pots, my arms up to my elbows in suds, ideas for songs would come into my head. I'd stack the dishwasher and when it whirred into action the sound of the gushing water and the mechanical motion would give me a sense of rhythm of the song I was composing. I'd stand there, tapping my foot to the beat of the rinse cycle, trying out the themes that came into my head.

I sang about what I knew and I sang from the heart. I told of the happiness that Tibetans shared at festivals, the sun shining on their faces as they sang and danced together, how there is an inner spirit active within us every second of every day, preparing us not only for this life but for the next as well. I told of the death of my mother when I was a child and sang for her peace. I sang of the yaks working in the fields with bells around their necks, and of the insects and worms that die during harvesting; I sang of mountains, rivers and meadows, of blue skies and rainbows. I sang of Tibetan pilgrimage, the slog of endless walking and climbing to holy places, and of the great blessings received in doing so. I sang of the great joy every Tibetan feels in seeing the Dalai Lama, even if only once in their life, and how when they gaze on his face it seems as though the sky is full of flowers. And I sang about the suffering of people all over the world in their search for peace and freedom and the responsibility each one of us has to bring love and peace into the world we live in.

It was not only Tibet that inspired me, however. On my way to and from the Masonic lodge I made friends with a seagull. I would listen to his song and whistle it back to him. Then he would reply. I would repeat it back to him and so it would go on, varying the tune a little each time. Every day for years the seagull waited for me after work and accompanied me home, flying just above my head, perching on fences and street corners until I had caught up with him. Later I made friends with a blackbird, and enjoyed singing with him as well. I treasured my friendships with these birds greatly.

In 2000 a very good English friend, Peta, who had been ordained as a Tibetan Buddhist nun and who loved my music, lent me some money so that I could make my own CD. I went down to the Church Road Studios in Hove, near Brighton, and recorded 11 songs, all my own compositions. On the front I put a photograph of myself as a young girl, taken shortly after I had escaped. In it I was wearing a purple dress against a backdrop of huge rugged mountains. I called the CD *The Unforgettable Land*. I had no producer or record company behind me; I simply sold it at my gigs and later from my website. Over time many people bought it and I began to get excellent reviews. Journalist Garth Cartwright wrote in the international world music magazine, *Froots*:

> When I received a copy of this album I was initially sniffy and doubted that a Tibetan effort from Brighton would impress me. How wrong could I get? Soname creates a haunted soundscape, one calling out to her beloved and brutalised homeland while offering spiritual accommodation. The music is largely conveyed by Soname's voice, an instrument that lifts notes out individually, strokes them and sets them free.

In the meantime I had started to experiment with fusion music, the blending of different genres of world music, which I found musically fascinating and more innovative than keeping to the pure strains of ethnic music alone. For this I began to bring in other musicians. Once again this got some encouraging reviews, as in this one from *Froots*:

Catching Soname in concert is an event: wearing traditional Tibetan dress she takes to the stage and begins to perform un-accompanied, her voice so powerful it almost overloads the speakers. Later she is joined by Phil Jackson on didgeridoo, Julian Franks on percussion and Eurick Adam on guitar.

Thrilled with how well my music was going, my friends in Brighton encouraged me to go for bigger goals. One particu-larly close friend English friend, Mark, suggested I send my CD to Andy Kershaw, the disc jockey well known for championing world music on the BBC. I had often listened to Andy's show, and thought highly of him. 'Please. He'll never listen to me. I don't have a record company. It's just my own CD. Just leave it alone,' I replied. 'No, no,' Mark persisted. 'You've got to try. Andy Kershaw is truly worthwhile. I happen to know his girlfriend works in a café in Crouch End, in north London. Let's go and find her and ask if she'll give Andy your CD. That way you'll have a much better chance than handing it into reception at the BBC where it will stay forgotten in a huge pile.'

That's what we did. We caught a train up to London and went looking for this girl around all the cafés in Crouch End. Finally we found the right place, but it was her day off. I handed the CD to another waitress, along with a covering letter, and asked her please to pass it on. I never thought she would, but what did I have to lose?

To my utter astonishment, a few days later the phone rang and it was Andy Kershaw's producer, saying that Andy would be playing my CD on the following Thursday night and also on his BBC World Service programme. I was astounded. On the Thursday Michael, Mark and I gathered around the radio to listen. I was literally shaking with excitement. Andy told his lis-teners about my escape and then said, 'Although her CD is not publicly available, Soname is fantastic to listen to.' Being recog-nised by Andy Kershaw boosted my confidence enormously. Convinced my music must be worth listening to, I became even more committed to a singing career.

On Saturday, 17 February 2001 I held my first solo gig at Brighton Komedia concert hall, in an auditorium holding hundreds of people. I had gained a lot of experience working with Geoff Smith, but I wanted the freedom to perform on my own, to be in charge of my own gigs. Like everything I had achieved in my life, I got the concert by simply going out there, knocking on doors, stepping into the unknown. I had approached the manager myself, handing him my CD, giving him a resumé of my concerts and press coverage, and he said he would be delighted for me to perform. I designed my own poster and put it up all over Brighton. The Komedia theatre ran a large advertisement in the local paper, with a picture of me on it, and the concert was a sell-out. I sang for two slots of 45 minutes each, separated by an interval. Holding the stage for that length of time by myself was a breakthrough and increased my confidence even further.

The concert led to more work, mostly at music festivals around the UK. For the first one I attended, I was horribly overdressed in my Tibetan *chuba*, and had to dash off to buy gypsy clothes. Most of the festivals I did for free, but I enjoyed doing them, and the experience and the exposure I gained were invaluable.

Not all my attempts to promote my singing career were equally successful. I had heard about the Barbican Concert Hall, in the City of London, and thought I'd try my hand at delivering a CD to them on the off-chance they would give me a concert as the Komedia had done. Normally Michael took me everywhere, as I got totally lost if I stepped a foot outside our front door. I can't follow directions at all and maps are a total mystery. To me, and every Tibetan, a map just looks like bird footprints. It was only when I was in a plane and looked down on the countryside beneath that I understood that roads looked like lines, and lakes like blue circles. But on this occasion Michael was away on a business trip to India and I decided it was about time I stopped relying on him and tried to find the Barbican by myself.

I knew how to get the Brighton train to Victoria Station in London, and decided I would ask my way from there. I'd negotiate the maze of tunnels of the Underground by putting down pebbles collected from Brighton beach, marking the route at each turn so I could find my way back again. This is what we do in Tibet. All went according to plan, and I successfully followed two businessmen to the Barbican, placing pebbles every few steps. The receptionist, however, would not take my CD and told me I would have to make an appointment. This one was too hard – I gave up!

I had better luck getting to Iceland. I had always been a great admirer of the Icelandic singer Björk and, in a modest way identified with her. She is tiny with a big voice, like me. She also comes from a small country yet has managed to bring her music to the whole world. By a stroke of great good fortune my friend Peta (who lent me the money to make my CD) knew Björk's manager, Arni Ben. Knowing I was a Björk fan, Peta kindly arranged for me to meet Arni when he was visiting her organic farm in Sussex with his family. We got on well and from that came an invitation to perform live in Iceland with Björk's former band, The Sugarcubes.

Although I had finally managed to get a one-year visa which technically allowed me to travel out of England, Iceland did not recognise my Yellow Travel Document and Arni had to arrange for police to meet me at the airport and let me in. Being without conventional official documents was making my life harder than I could possibly have guessed. But once there I fell in love with Iceland. I was surprised to find it was not covered in ice, but was mostly green; I was told that Greenland, on the other hand, is mostly ice!

The concert itself went extremely well. Many journalists came, and I made the front page of the main newspaper. Arni phoned to congratulate me. He told me they hadn't heard my kind of music before and that the audience was delighted by my performance.

It was not intentional, but through my songs and the publicity I was attracting, I was becoming an ambassador for my country. 'You are singing for Tibet,' my friends in Brighton told me. 'No I'm not, I'm singing for myself,' I replied. But they insisted, saying 'That's not the case.' And slowly it dawned on me that because of my appearance, how I introduced my songs, and what I was saying in my interviews I *was* representing Tibet, whether I meant to or not. When people came up to me in the street and said, 'You're the Tibetan singer, we saw your concert. Thank you,' I would feel embarrassed because I felt I did not deserve praise or fame. Without the respect and love His Holiness the Dalai Lama has gathered from his travels all over the world, nobody would be interested in Tibet. And where would I be if Tibet was not suffering? I certainly would not be in the West, let alone singing, and no one would have heard of me.

But if my strange, erratic life had somehow led me to become a singer, with growing public exposure, then I was more than willing to use my voice to help Tibet in any way I could. I had found myself in a kind of paradise, with so many opportunities. I had even learnt to swim! So how could I bask in all that I had gained when I knew Tibet was still suffering? My people were gagged, but I could sing for them.

Sometimes Western people would relate their problems to me. When I told them what I had gone through and explained the plight of Tibet, they would often say it helped them put their own lives in perspective. Acutely aware of the freedom I now enjoyed, whenever I could I walked rather than took the bus and bought clothes from charity shops, sending the money I had saved to Tibetan causes.

And I was delighted to sing for Tibet, whenever I was asked. This led me to meet the actress Joanna Lumley. Joanna was brought up in India, while her grandparents had been to Tibet, and she had long been a fan of the Dalai Lama and Buddhism. A dedicated supporter of the Free Tibet Campaign, she was hosting a fundraising event at which I was invited to perform. To be truthful, the name Joanna Lumley meant nothing to me. It was only later, when Michael told me that I had watched her several times in *Absolutely Fabulous*, that I realised who she was.

The concert was held in a beautiful Grade II listed house in West London, the home of a wealthy Indian family. Joanna was beautifully dressed. Many people came and we made £10,000. Two months later she put on another concert in aid of Tibet, this time in a special music room in the garden of her own home, and asked me to perform again. Joanna dressed in a Tibetan *chuba* and provided all the food and drink herself. Another £10,000 was raised; it went mainly to help political prisoners, including the nuns incarcerated in the female wing of Lhasa's notorious Drapchi prison. Joanna read out the moving words of Passang Lhamo, a Tibetan nun jailed for peacefully protesting against Chinese rule. She had written a terrible account of the beatings and torture she and many other nuns endured, reporting that she had seen several fellow inmates die. It's not widely known, but Tibetan nuns have been ferociously brave in leading demonstrations for religious freedom.

All prisoners in Tibet have a terrible time. Usually their only 'crime' is that they have followed the Dalai Lama or have campaigned for Tibet's freedom. They may be fed human excrement and many are tortured and beaten until they are paralysed and near death; then their families are told to come and take them away so that they do not die in prison. Sometimes they are shot and the family not only has to come and take the body away but pay for the bullet too.

That is real suffering. These crimes are never reported, so few in the outside world are aware of what is going on in Tibet. I think people are frightened of China and its commercial power. When you have so much material comfort as we do in the West, you can become blind to the suffering of others. That, in its way, is another sort of prison.

On 23 November 2003 came my greatest chance yet to perform for my country when I was asked to sing at a gala at the Royal Opera House, in London's Covent Garden, in aid of the Tibet Relief Fund. The tickets cost £130 each and the money raised was going to help the Tibetan refugee communities.

Titled 'An Evening for Tibet', the event was supported by an impressive line-up of celebrities including Prince Charles, Mick Jagger, Richard Gere, Annie Lennox, Clive Anderson, Ruby Wax and many more, as well as Joanna Lumley. I was billed to sing alongside the brilliant British soprano Lesley Garrett, but at the last minute she got flu and was replaced by Yvonne Kenny, the Australian diva.

As usual I had no idea who she was, nor what or where the Royal Opera House was. I lived in a small Brighton flat and worked as a cleaner – what did I know of opera singers? When I casually told Michael what I was doing he exclaimed, 'You don't realise how important the Royal Opera House is! It's where Britain's greatest operas and ballets are performed. Stars come from all over the world to perform there. It's a great honour to be asked.' My head was not turned. 'So what?' I replied. 'I'm singing not for myself, for my own ego, but for Tibet.' I did not think it was right to charge even for my own travel expenses – and I paid for Michael's ticket too.

When the evening came I put on a bronze *chuba* with black flowers, wore long coral earrings and an amber, turquoise and silver necklace and let my hair hang loose. I was not at all nervous when I stepped up to sing but the audience looked very uptight and stiff in their black jackets, bow ties and long evening gowns. I have to loosen them up, I thought. 'You all look wonderful in your posh clothes but you also seem a little tense. Why not shake your arms a little, enjoy yourselves? This is for Tibet,' I said.

They began to grin. There is nothing like singing to make people feel happy, and so I taught them the mantra of Tibet, the beloved mantra of compassion, *om mani padme hum*, which I had said to myself over and over again during my escape, and got them to sing it to me. To hear the Floral Hall of the Royal Opera House, that bastion of Western culture, reverberate with the sacred sound was wonderful. It certainly relaxed the audience. After that I sang a song I had composed myself called 'Vulnerable', about my longing to return to Tibet:

I will sing once again
Under the mountain tree
And raindrops will beat a rhythm
On its leaves
I will return
To see the cool spring again

It was a special night. There was a delicious meal, champagne and dancing before I took the last train back to Brighton and our one-bedroom flat.

The very next day I got up early, as usual, said my prayers and began my cleaning shift at the police station. I still needed the money to make ends meet, because in spite of my growing fame I was still hard up. My life was strange. One minute I was singing at the Royal Opera House, mixing with aristocrats, being a star, the next I was emptying wastepaper baskets, duster in hand. The ramifications of my Royal Opera House performance, however, rippled on. The *Observer* did a full-page spread on me under the heading 'From Cleaning Lady to Leading Lady'. They photographed me in an apron and trainers with a broom sweeping an office floor and printed it next to a picture of the plush interior of the Opera House.

The gala itself was filmed by the BBC and sent around the world. Later I heard that people in Dharamsala, including my old girlfriend Dolma, had actually seen it. I also appeared in colour in the *Sunday Telegraph* magazine, where it was said of my performance: 'In a beautiful voice so clear it sounds like she could shatter glass, she sings about her life in Tibet and the folk songs she loved as a child.' That was nice. And I did interviews for radio stations in Denmark, Switzerland, the USA and Germany. Along with many admiring telephone calls and emails, I even received £50 from someone in Switzerland.

All the publicity further boosted my singing career. After the Opera House I was asked to perform at festivals in Europe as well as in Britain. I sang in Malaga, Spain, at a festival featuring many sorts of music – rock and roll, jazz, world music. I liked

southern Spain, although after England the weather was too hot
for me. I went to Macugnaga in Piedmont, northern Italy, to
take part in the annual mountain festival of Saint Bernardo and
was thrilled to win the Best Performer award, the first prize I
had ever won in my entire life. My performance was broadcast
by national TV.

From total obscurity my face was becoming well known
throughout the world – except in Tibet. My family would have
no idea what had become of me, nor of the extraordinary life I
was now leading. I liked to think that my mother, grandparents
and siblings would have been proud of what I had achieved from
my own efforts, without any education and from such a terrible
start. I was not so sure about my father's reaction! Would I still
have been a performing monkey to him?

The greatest accolade of my singing career to date came
when I was asked to perform at the Dalai Lama's World Peace
Ceremony, at the Usher Hall, Edinburgh, during which the
Dalai Lama himself gave an inspiring address about the raising
of a compassionate new generation. Afterwards he came up to
me and spoke. 'Where are you from? Are you newly come from
Tibet?' he asked. I could hardly speak, I was trembling so much.
'I am from Yarlung, but I spent some time in India before coming here,' I managed to say.

Being that close to His Holiness, he seemed extraordinarily
big, but I think that was due more to his presence than his
height. He was somehow strong and yet tender, like a baby. I felt
blissfully happy and dreadfully inadequate at the same time. I
could sense the love and kindness pouring out of him, but I also
felt he could see right through me into the core of my very
being. It was not a comfortable feeling. I need to do much more
purification practice, I thought, then I would be worthy of
standing before the Dalai Lama. If I were a yogini who had done
years of sincere meditation maybe I would be able to benefit
from being in his presence, and my spiritual growth would take
a gigantic leap. There and then I renewed the lay person's vows
that I had taken at the Kalachakra initiation in Spiti all those

years ago and determined to make more effort with my meditation practice. Tentatively, I gave him my prayer beads and humbly asked if he would bless them. Without hesitation he took them, said mantras over them and blew on them. A month later I was still shaking.

CHAPTER FOURTEEN

Reunion

IMAY HAVE BEEN BUSY with my flourishing singing career, attracting media attention, but my daughter was constantly in my thoughts and I had never given up hope that I would find her again. With this in mind I had opened a bank account for her, and I regularly put into it whatever spare money I had. It was an exercise in positive thinking, and the only thing I could do. I still had no idea where she was, or what she was doing.

Unbeknown to me, however, the forces of karma were at work. One day in the autumn of 2002, I was talking to a Tibetan friend in London when she mentioned someone who was escorting Tibetan refugees to New York. 'I know this man from my Dharamsala days,' I said in delight. 'I'd love to talk to him. Can you give me his phone number?'

When I rang him in the USA, he was very kind. 'This will be costing you a fortune. I'll call you back immediately,' he said. We had a long conversation, and I asked if he ever saw Tenzin. Since my last disastrous phone call in Delhi, I had had no contact with him at all. After his absolute refusal to talk to me on that occasion I was too nervous to call him again. Like his parents, Tenzin obviously thought I was a wicked woman. And, I have to admit, I still harboured feelings of guilt at letting Deckyi go. But time had passed and I thought maybe now he would be more forthcoming and understanding. My old friend told me he saw Tenzin occasionally at Tibetan functions and that he would get his new phone number for me. He called me back with Tenzin's details just half an hour later.

I plucked up courage and dialled. When a woman answered the phone, I introduced myself as 'an old friend' who wanted to speak to Tenzin. She told me she was Tenzin's wife and that he was not in, but to call back later. When I did she picked up the phone again, saying Tenzin was still out. I came clean and told her who I was, explaining that I had only called to find out about my daughter. It was clear that Tenzin's wife, who was also Tibetan, knew about me and Deckyi. 'All I can tell you,' she said, 'is that she is in a school in India. I dare not tell you any more because it will get me into trouble with Tenzin. You must talk to him yourself. But please do your very best to contact her because Tenzin hasn't seen her since he left. You are her mother and I think she needs you.'

Her words sent a chill down my spine. Was my greatest fear – that Deckyi had been damaged by my leaving her – going to prove true? I rang New York a third time and finally managed to catch Tenzin. 'Please, tell me about my daughter. Where is she? What has happened to her?' I begged.

Once again, he said nothing. There was silence down the line. But I had learnt my lesson. This time I didn't hang up in despair as I had before, I just kept asking about Deckyi. He didn't want to tell me anything; eventually, though, after I repeated my questions several times, he told me what I already knew, that she was in India. 'But I don't want you to have any contact with her. Leave her alone. Her education in India is almost finished and then I'm going to bring her to the USA.' There was a pause before he added, 'You know, my family in Tibet had many expenses looking after Deckyi. It wasn't easy for them. I've sent a lot of money to Tibet and India over the years, to help support my family and Deckyi. Now I'm really hard up.'

Wow, I thought, he just wants money. But after my initial

shock I realised that, in a way, he had a point. I had contributed nothing to Deckyi's education or upbringing – not because I didn't want to, but because I did not know where she was. If that was all it was going to take to find my daughter, it was OK by me. I took his address and as soon as I could sent him £1,500, all the money I had managed to save for Deckyi. In return he gave me her address and phone number. It was the greatest exchange I had ever made.

I found out no more about her – how she was or how she had ended up back in India. All I knew was that she was at a Tibetan government school in Mussorie, another former British hill station in the Indian Himalaya, a 14-hour bus journey south-east of Dharamsala. 'When you call, don't tell her who you are. It will be too big a shock,' were Tenzin's parting words. It was the last conversation I ever had with him.

I looked at the number in my hand and without another moment's hesitation, I dialled. It had been nine years since I had last heard my daughter's voice. Miraculously the lines in India were not down as usual. I got straight through to the school and asked for Deckyi. She came on to the line and, trying to control my voice, I did as Tenzin had instructed, introducing myself as 'a friend of your mother, calling from Tibet'.

Like her father, she hardly said a word. I rattled on, asking lots of questions: 'How are you doing? What is your school like?' I could tell she was puzzled at this weird woman asking all these questions, and she answered in monosyllables.

Then I made a mistake. 'What size shoe do you take?' I asked, using the English word 'size', which no one in Tibet could possibly know. Instantly she realised that I definitely was not who I said I was and clammed up completely. My heart was wrenched wide open – all I had wanted was to send her a new pair of shoes. Deckyi was so close and yet emotionally, as well as geographically, impossibly far away. I was a total stranger to her and did not know how to reach out to her. I could feel the tears welling up, but I kept my voice bright until I put the phone down. Then I sobbed and sobbed on Michael's shoulder.

'Patience,' he said patting me on the shoulder. 'Soon, when your legal papers are in order, you can go and see her, and it will be better,' he said.

But my karma with Deckyi was far from over. All the time I had been in England I had kept in touch with Alfred Rover, a German whom I had met while living in Delhi. He had been very kind to me, on one occasion sending me 6,000 rupees – an amount so shockingly enormous to me that I immediately sent it back to him. Alfred had been actively involved in helping the Tibetans ever since they first arrived in India, back in 1959, and he was an old friend of the Dalai Lama. By an extraordinary stroke of fate, he was a sponsor of Deckyi's school.

I decided to explain my situation to him and ask if he would meet Deckyi when he next went to Mussorie, take her out to dinner and tell her who I was. I knew she was confused about the woman who had unexpectedly phoned her. Alfred, I believed, would be the best person to break it to her gently that her mother was alive and well, living in England and thinking about her. He succeeded in carrying out this delicate mission, and reported back that Deckyi was a lovely girl, popular at school, but that she had seemed unable to grasp what he was telling her. He also told me he had a recent photograph of her, which he was going to send me.

I waited with exquisite anticipation to see the daughter I had not laid eyes on for nine years. When the letter came I tore it open and there in front of my eyes was a head-and-shoulders photograph of a beautiful young girl, with a heart-shaped face and full lips slightly turned up in an enigmatic smile. Her hair was parted in the middle and she wore a Western-style school uniform of white blouse, striped tie and V-necked sweater. I looked at her finely boned face, and thought I recognised her father's face in her. (To be truthful, I saw little of myself!) The photograph became my most treasured possession. I fingered it so much it became creased and torn at the corners.

The next year, 2003, another one-year visa was stamped into my Yellow Travel Document, which meant I could leave England and hopefully return without too much difficulty. There was nothing now stopping me from seeing my daughter. With the school's permission I made arrangements to spend ten days with Deckyi in Dharamsala – time enough, I hoped, for us to get reacquainted without the meeting being too drawn out.

In June I boarded another Aeroflot plane before retracing my steps from Delhi to Dharamsala, where a teacher was bringing Deckyi to meet me at the Drepung Oselling hotel. I was already very nervous and the journey had not started well. Aeroflot lost my suitcase, containing not only my clothes but all the presents I had bought for Deckyi. I had had such pleasure choosing them – little tops, books, and shoes – and was devastated that I now had nothing to give her. I knew first hand what it meant to receive a gift, never having had one as a child. On that long overnight bus journey I prayed that my daughter was looking forward to our reunion as much as I was. But I dared not hope too much. We had been parted for so long, and who knew what she really felt about me.

At 6.30 am, the bus juddered to a halt. I immediately raced to the hotel – to be told, to my dismay, that it was completely full and there was not a single room for me to book into. I had forgotten that June and July were the height of the holiday season, when many Indians got married and headed for the hills to get out of the intense heat for their honeymoon. I began to panic. How were Deckyi and I ever going to find each other? I ran to several nearby hotels to see if she had booked in, but she hadn't. There were no vacancies anywhere. I dashed back to the bus station in the centre of town to see if a young girl was waiting there. My stomach was knotting with anxiety, my mouth was dry. I ran through the crowds of people milling about the bus station but could not see anyone who looked like Deckyi's photograph.

After two or three frantic, fruitless hours of searching, a Tibetan whom I had passed several times approached and asked if I had just come from England. It was Deckyi's teacher. With him was a girl aged 13, with short thick hair. 'Here is your child,' he said.

Before me stood an extremely beautiful, slim girl much taller than I had anticipated. It took me by surprise – her photograph had given no indication of her height. 'Ah, she definitely takes after her father,' I thought, recalling that Tenzin was nearly six feet tall. We stood in the bus station looking at each other, saying nothing. I had waited so long for this moment, and now that it had finally arrived, my emotions were so intense and turbulent that I did not know what to do. Throwing my arms around her was definitely not the right thing – Tibetans never approve of public displays of affection, and in my situation it was utterly inappropriate. She was accompanied by another young girl of the same age whom she introduced as Dolga, her sister. I was taken aback, but I said nothing.

To break the ice I focused on the practical. 'Go and see if you can find us a room in this guesthouse – mention my name,' I told Dolga, remembering a place that was run by a former friend of mine. 'We will wait here for you.'

Having delivered Deckyi, her teacher had returned to the school, and now Deckyi and I were left alone. We sat on a big stone at the side of the road, and I looked down at her feet. To my horror I saw that her shoes were too small for her and were coming apart – that broke my heart. I was so angry that my suitcase had been lost. 'I bought new shoes for you in England – they are coming later,' I began, somewhat lamely. Her silence continued. 'You know, I really am your mother,' I blurted out, extracting from my handbag some old photographs of Deckyi and me taken in Dharamsala when she was very little. I wanted to offer absolute proof of my identity, as she obviously did not recognise me at all.

Deckyi glanced at the pictures, but still looked uncertain. 'Please understand, I hated parting from you, but I couldn't afford to look after you. I had no choice,' I began. But the bus depot was no place for such a conversation, and Deckyi did not say a word. I understood. How could she feel anything but extremely uncomfortable having a stranger announce that she was her mother?

Dolga returned with the news that there was a vacancy in the guesthouse. The next few days were strange, the three of us living together in one room while I tried to get to know Deckyi. Gradually I pieced together a little of what had happened to her after she had left me in Delhi. Her grandparents had taken her back to Tibet, as they said they would, and settled her with her aunt, her father's sister, who had a daughter just a few months older. This was Dolga. I heard that from the beginning Deckyi had been taught to call her aunt 'mother', and over the years that was what she had become in Deckyi's mind. No one ever told her that she had a real mother living in India. In fact no one talked about me at all. Over time I had been successfully erased from my daughter's awareness.

What I had surmised was brutally true – to Tenzin's family I was a bad woman, an unfit mother, and Deckyi was better off knowing nothing about me at all. Tenzin's cold, utterly uncommunicative manner towards me was now perfectly clear. He was part of the policy to cut me out of Deckyi's life completely. I was devastated. Every child needs to know about their real mother and father, even if they are not physically present.

Never one to give up, I persisted in trying to break through her resistance. 'Did you ever think that your auntie was not your mother?' I asked. 'I called her mother, but I felt something was wrong,' Deckyi admitted quietly. And in a complete turn-around, both she and Dolga now began to call me 'mother'. I had longed to hear Deckyi say it, but in this context it did not bring the joy I had hoped for.

As I had suspected, Deckyi had run into problems when she reached school age. Being Indian born, she did not have the required certification to qualify her for a Tibetan state education. Not knowing what to do, her relatives had paid a businessman to take both Deckyi and Dolga illegally across the border to Nepal and India, where they were enrolled in the Mussorie school. In sending both girls to India they were thinking of Dolga as much as Deckyi – they wanted their daughter to benefit from an Indian education, which they knew was superior to a Tibetan one. Still, I appreciated the fact that the girls were not separated and that Dolga's mother came to see them as often as she could, which sadly was only every other year.

The girls talked, allowing me to put together the pieces of the jigsaw, and it dawned on me that Deckyi had actually returned to India a few months before I left to go to France and England. For those few months we had been on the same continent together, and I had not known. True to form, no one had told me. That was bitter news to swallow, but I tried to keep mending fences.

'Were you sad because your mum and dad left you behind? It must have been hard for you being alone at school in India all this time – not having any mother and father,' I managed to ask. 'Not really, all the kids at school are in the same position. Either their parents have spilt up, or they are orphans, or their parents are back in Tibet,' Deckyi replied nonchalantly, which put my mind at rest a little. I also discovered that her father phoned her occasionally, but that he had never seen her since the day he walked out on her and me. How could he do that? He knew where she was all the time, and yet he had not bothered to make the journey from America to see his own daughter. It was incomprehensible to me. The moment I knew where Deckyi was, I wanted to rush to her side.

Deckyi was a lovely girl, I learnt. She liked school, she was musical and played Tibetan instruments (like her grandfather), she could cook (unlike her mother), she was popular and had a reputation for being very good with the younger children. How could Tenzin not want to know her?

The girls were still inseparable, but their characters were very different. Dolga was friendly, outgoing and talkative, even showing signs of affection towards me. Deckyi, in contrast, was silent, remote and apathetic, at least in my company. This worried me. She seemed to have little zest for life. This was so unlike the vivacious, cheeky daughter I had known, who made friends with all the local storekeepers and who at two years old had boldly wandered off on her own to visit a friend who lived away down several winding, tiny alleyways. I had been demented with fear but finally found her perfectly well and happy in my friend's house.

This older Deckyi was decidedly conservative, again unlike her mother. 'Please, braid your hair, don't wear it loose. And don't wear trousers – put on a Tibetan *chuba*,' she told me. She was very Tibetan. She insisted on covering herself up in spite of the heat. I didn't know if she was always like this, or if it was just with me. Maybe she really is a little bit scarred inside, I thought with sorrow. Maybe she is just a teenager. Maybe she is seething with anger and resentment. Maybe she is confused. I was in the dark. I had no expertise in how girls of that age behave, while I myself had been forced virtually into an adult existence since the age of six.

I kept trying to get close to her, to forge some bond between us, but it was impossible in that artificial situation while the two girls were together all the time. The last thing I wanted to do was create any rift between them by favouring Deckyi in any way, or taking her aside. If it were hard for my daughter it was excruciatingly difficult for me. As the ten days wore on I became increasingly disappointed and frustrated. Our reunion was not going remotely as I had imagined. It did not help that in order to retrieve my suitcase, which had finally been found, I had to make the horrendous bus journey back to Delhi in the intense summer heat. Deckyi seemed only marginally pleased with the gifts I had bought her, but by that stage I was so totally worn out that I did not have the energy to be upset.

By the end of the reunion I was physically exhausted and emotionally drained. The teacher came and took the girls back to Mussorie. There was no possibility of our staying together at this stage. Deckyi had to return to school, which was what I most wanted anyway. 'The only thing I want you to do for me is to get an education, because your mum is not educated. It will make me very happy. No pressure, just do the best you can,' I told her. I had to go back to England, to Michael and my singing and cleaning jobs. In order to help Deckyi, I had to get on with my life and earn money.

After they had gone I was left with conflicting emotions. It had been a difficult time. I had found my daughter physically, but not emotionally. She certainly had not seemed pleased to have found me. I didn't know what the future held, or what I could or should do. Perhaps she wanted nothing more to do with me. I sat at the bus stop in Dharamsala, waiting for the bus to take me back to Delhi, and cried. And from my heart I prayed to the female Buddha Tara, born out of the tears of the Buddha, who rushes to help those in distress. Tara is very powerful. 'Please Tara, both my daughter and I have been through so much. Help me to be strong now.'

Back in England, I phoned Deckyi regularly, asking how she was and catching up on the news. Often I spoke to Dolga, who was still more willing to communicate, rather than Deckyi. I sent Deckyi pocket money every month via the school, asking her to share it with her cousin. It came to 100 rupees a week, enough to buy sweets and a few extras – not much, but infinitely more than I ever had.

Although in one way it was the most incredible relief to be in touch with Deckyi again, at the same time it was torture. My daughter was now back in my life and I would never know the same freedom as I had when I was ignorant of her whereabouts and welfare. Now, Deckyi shared every waking moment with me. If I ate a piece of chocolate, I thought how much Deckyi would enjoy it. If I went to a nice park I imagined how Deckyi would respond. When I went shopping for clothes I wished my daughter were with me so that we could go through the racks together. I could never be totally selfish again.

I dreamt that one day Deckyi would be able to join me in England and taste some of the freedom and opportunities that I now enjoyed. But that choice was up to her and the British government. If I did not get citizenship, she could never join me, whether she wanted to or not.

Admittedly the prospect of having my daughter with me permanently wasn't all rosy. The responsibility of taking on a teenage daughter with a difficult past was daunting. I was afraid, too, that I might let her down again. I suspected she had suffered emotional damage and I did not want to make it any worse. Taking this into account I decided not to have another child. I discussed it with Michael: 'If I make more babies, my time will be taken up by them and then, if Deckyi comes to live with us, she will feel left out all over again. Being born in England, the new child will have all the security and opportunities that she never had. I couldn't bear to do that to her.' Michael agreed. He said he was too old to be a new father and Deckyi would be enough.

He was such a good man, and for all our cultural differences, our bond was very strong. It was a sensible decision, but deep in my being I yearned for the warmth, support and love of a family of my own. I had been without blood ties for so long.

CHAPTER FIFTEEN

Blood Ties

TARA, THE FEMALE BUDDHA, whom I had implored for help with Deckyi, must still have been listening to my prayers. One night around midnight when I returned home, very tired, from singing at a folk festival in Wales, Michael told me I had a letter from China. 'That's not possible. I don't know anyone in China,' I replied. But when I looked at the letter, sure enough there was a Chinese stamp on it. Curious, I opened it. All it said was: 'I am your younger sister, Lakchung Dorga, and this is my telephone number.'

I stood looking at the letter, utterly astonished. I had neither seen nor heard from my little sister since my escape from Tibet over 16 years ago. She was ten years younger than me, born when I was living in Lhasa, and I had only seen her twice in my life. How on earth had she found me?

As usual, I acted immediately. Without thinking what time it was, I dialled the number written before me. The phone was answered by a woman – it was Lakchung Dorga herself. We were both so overcome with tears of happiness that neither of us could say anything except 'Hello.' 'For years we didn't know if you were alive or dead,' she sobbed.

Thrilled beyond measure at finding my sister after so long, I called several times over the next few weeks. Countless aunts, uncles and cousins were summoned to the telephone to say hello, upon which they would usually burst into tears. Our telephone bill for that quarter came to £600. I didn't care. A miracle had happened. It was as though my family had come back from the dead.

I learnt that my sister was now in Lhasa, married to a doctor of Tibetan medicine. (Of course, I realised, Tibet now used Chinese stamps!) She already had a little girl a year old and was a skilled worker at a carpet factory. She told me that ten girls could finish an intricate design in three months, though for all this the money was poor. My father and brothers were still in Yarlung, my brothers both married with children, and farming. My father, I was told, was getting old, and was unsteady on his feet. Recently he had fallen down the stairs and hurt himself badly. They had taken him to hospital where they had to deposit a large sum of money before he would be admitted and treated. This didn't sound like Communism to me. What happened if you were poor or unemployed? Even our National Health Service was better than that.

It was the same with international phone calls. In Tibet you had to pay the post office a vast amount before making the call, and they would refund you what you hadn't spent. But in my country, I discovered thankfully, I could use phone cards which only cost me 1p a minute.

From my side I told her about my marriage, my singing and my daughter, but not in much detail. I certainly said nothing about my escape or my time in Dharamsala. I knew the phones were tapped and any mention of the Dalai Lama or escaping would have landed my family in big trouble. Instead we kept to the safe topic of family affairs – which suited me fine. I was hungry for family news.

My sister had tracked me down from the very occasional letters I wrote to my father when I arrived first in Delhi and then England. I did not tell him much, I just wanted him to know where I was and that I was well. As I'd given them to travellers going to Tibet and had never received a reply, I assumed they had never reached him. But he had got every one, and had tucked them all behind the wooden beam holding up the roof of his house. When Lakchung Dorga heard that her father-in-law was going to Delhi on business she immediately asked to see the letters so she could give him my address. That's when she discovered I had gone to England. The precious letter that landed in Brighton was the result.

My karma had ripened once more, in the most wonderful way. For years my daughter and my family had been lost to me, and then within a few short months I had found them both. Nothing is fixed, the Buddha said, everything is subject to change. Having made contact I now yearned for us all to be together once more – to see each other in the flesh, to catch up on all the years that had passed, to be a living, active family again.

By late 2004 I was finally granted British residency and was legally allowed to travel abroad. Through a series of complicated arrangements I organised for Deckyi, Dolga, my sister and her family to meet me in Delhi. My idea was that we should go on pilgrimage to Bodhgaya in Bihar, the place where the Buddha attained enlightenment, and then on to Dharamsala, where the Dalai Lama was giving teachings in his temple. I couldn't think of a better way for us all to get to know each other. I borrowed £1,000 from the bank and flew off in December 2004 for the grand family reunion.

I walked through the winding alleyways of Majnu Katilla, the Tibetan colony of Delhi, where we had arranged to meet, my heart pounding with anticipation. I was so excited at the thought that I was about to see my sister again. What would she be like? Would we have anything in common, having led such radically different lives? I longed to see Deckyi again too, and prayed that it would be a little easier this time.

We had agreed that they would all assemble and wait for me in a flat above a small grocer's store. And as I walked through the door, there was a squeal of delight. My heart jumped – this was a wonderful welcome. A small woman with long hair, who could only be Lakchung Dorga, ran across the room, threw her arms around me and kissed me. As I embraced her I was instantly transported back to Yarlung and was in my mother's arms once more. She was as stunningly beautiful as the day she was born, when my father named her after a goddess. She was also wearing jeans, a T-shirt and make-up, which took me aback. I didn't expect her to look so Western. She's a product of modern Tibet, I thought.

My reception from Deckyi was still cool, although Dolga came over and gave me a hug. But the room was such a scene of happy pandemonium that I hadn't time to dwell on my daughter's attitude. Into a very small space were crammed Lakchung's father-in-law, her neighbours from Lhasa, a woman friend and the owners of the house, as well as my daughter, my sister and Dolga.

The next morning we all set off on our pilgrimage, as Tibetans have done for centuries, revelling in sharing a spiritual quest and being together. And as on every pilgrimage we sang, but this time to my songs which I had brought with me on the CD I had cut, *The Unforgettable Land*. Everyone seemed quite impressed, and I noticed as they sang along that my sister had an excellent voice.

The following weeks were rich in every way. Bodhgaya was special beyond anything I had imagined. Even 2,500 years after the Buddha attained enlightenment there, sitting under the Bodhi tree, you could still feel the spiritual power of that great event. Bodhgaya had become a dirty, dusty place, full of beggars, but nevertheless the soil itself seemed holy and the air was infused with a kind of purity. I am walking where the Buddha himself walked, I thought in awe.

Lakchung and I got on extremely well. Every morning I woke up excited that she was with me. I loved her company. She was a peaceful woman, very feminine and refined, like our mother. She had brought letters from my brothers, who sent their love along with words to the effect of 'I bet you are as madcap as ever!' It was great to hear from them. She told me about life in contemporary Tibet. I hardly recognised it. I heard that women were now bleaching their skin to make them fairer, white skin being considered more desirable than their natural Tibetan tan. This was deeply shocking. So was the news that the nomads were no longer allowed to roam with their livestock, but were being herded into small prescribed areas, with the result that their yaks and sheep were dying from insufficient food.

Tibet itself was dying. She said that finding a job was harder than ever unless you were Chinese (who came at the head of the queue) or could bribe the top man with a refrigerator or a big TV. Youngsters drank too much because they were dispossessed. And farmers, like my brothers, had to take on extra work so that they could afford to send their children to school. Every school in Tibet was now fee paying.

The picture she painted grew bleaker the more she talked. Religion was allowed but only on a superficial level. Prayers were permitted but teaching the profound understanding of the mind, the very hallmark of Tibetan Buddhism that entails using your own wisdom, was prohibited. There was no freedom of speech or information. If you indulged in any political activity you were given hell. If you stole or raped you were given a light sentence, but if you talked about the Dalai Lama or protested peacefully you were tortured and thrown in jail for decades. It was a grim picture and my heart bled anew. The suffering of my people seemed endless.

In turn I told her of all the tragic things that had happened to me, and she cried. 'Poor thing, you have been through a lot. It must have been hell – and we weren't there to support you,' she commiserated. I asked her, 'Do you remember Mother at all?' She replied that she did not. Her answer was telling. While Lakchung had been nearly four when our mother had died, Deckyi had been less than three when I gave her to her grand-parents. She could have no memory of me. It helped me under-stand her behaviour much better.

All the time we were travelling Deckyi remained fairly

uncommunicative, often preferring to stay in the hotel room watching TV with Dolga rather than join us as we visited the sites where the Buddha had meditated and taught. Sometimes she even got Dolga to speak for her. 'You can't force the relationship. Give her time,' my sister advised, seeing how upset I would become over Deckyi's behaviour.

I decided she was right. Maybe it was the fact that we were in Bodhgaya, surrounded by the influence of the holy places where the Buddha had been, but I gradually began to become more pragmatic. After all, the Buddha taught detachment as a major component in finding peace. I realised that Deckyi had her own suffering, just like every single person on the planet, and she had to work through that. That is how we all grow and learn. I could not take her suffering from her, in the same way as no one can take away my suffering from me. Thinking like this made me feel better. I will give Deckyi all I can, I thought. And if she rejects me I will be devastated, but I will cope because I am strong.

After a month in Bodhgaya, I had to take Deckyi and Dolga back to school. Afterwards I arranged to meet up with my sister and her party in Dharamsala to receive the Dalai Lama's teachings. They had, of course, no idea how extraordinary he was and they were all bowled over by his immense spiritual presence. Religious seeds that had lain dormant began to sprout. 'Now I know why you wake up every morning and meditate,' my sister commented.

Thousands had come to hear him teach from near and far – it was a gathering that used to happen regularly in Tibet, but no longer. I realised then that Tibet's great loss had been the world's gain. If the Chinese had not invaded, if the Dalai Lama had not gone into exile, then no one outside Tibet would ever have benefited from this remarkable man and all that he had to teach us in the way of wisdom and compassion.

Having been to Bodhgaya, having sat in front of the Dalai Lama every day for four weeks, I began to think how good it would be if I could go on a long retreat. Singing was enjoyable

– it brought me an income and, I hope, gave others pleasure – but in the long run I believed there was nothing more worthwhile to do with your life than to foster your spiritual nature. What else can you take with you when you die? Nothing develops your spirituality faster than retreat, as those amazing yogis and meditators in Tibet had shown. Even though I had been born during the Cultural Revolution, my Tibetan heritage was alive and well, it seemed. For me, the proof of a successful retreat would be an increase in love. To my mind, if you do not develop the heart none of the religious teachings mean anything. It was kindness, compassion and love that made it all worthwhile.

While I was in Dharamsala, supported by my sister, I decided it was time to find Ngawang Panchen, the torch-bearing monk who had helped me escape, and who had carried me when I could no longer walk over the mountains and was prepared to die. I had not dared contact him before, because I was wary of what he would think of my having Deckyi so soon after escaping, of being abandoned and my scandalous affair that had blackened my name. But many years had passed, and I longed to see him again. A few enquiries brought me to the Nechung Monastery, home of the famous Nechung Oracle, a monk who goes into trance and proffers State advice to the Dalai Lama. Ngawang Panchen was there, still a monk, and a very serious practitioner. I was so happy that he hadn't wavered from his path in all these years. So many escapee monks had – the dislocation they experienced, together with the materialism they found in India, proving too much for their vows.

It was good to see him. We sat down and talked, going over that incredible journey we had made together. From this distance in time it seemed unreal, as though it had never happened. We reminisced about all the hardships we had endured, and laughed at the time when I got lost because I stayed behind to go to the toilet. But it had happened and we were each other's witnesses to what we had gone through. We shared a unique history and I knew the bond between us would never be broken. I harboured a secret dream that one day I would be able to invite him to England to talk about his life and the special role of the Nechung Oracle.

By the time the holiday came to an end and we had to return to our respective lives, I was extremely close to my sister and felt a terrible wrench when we said our goodbyes. She cried too. I felt in my bones, however, that somewhere we would see each other again. When I got back to England I called her and she told me our father had died while we had all been together in India.

It had been a special death, she said. In the past few years he had resumed his life as a monk in his former monastery, which had been partially rebuilt. The day before he passed away he had visited all his old friends to wish them well and thank them for all they had done. 'What are you talking about? You look in good health. We'll see you soon,' they said. But he knew. His years of meditation told him his time had come. My sister said he died with a sublime expression on his face, a sign that he would have a good rebirth. Hearing the news I felt indescribably sad. If only he could have been a little warmer towards me, more demonstrative, we could have had a better relationship. Now it would never be.

My father wasn't the only man who was departing from my life. After my return from my family reunion Michael announced he wanted to sell the flat, buy a house in Goa, India, the country he loved, and travel around. This threw me. I didn't want to go back and live in India at all. England had become my home. It was where I had my singing career. I loved England – the weather, the lifestyle, the mental freedom, the social ease. I appreciated it even more, having just spent several weeks in India. England had value systems I respected and admired – like the way people with physical and mental disabilities are treated with kindness. Life for disabled people in the East is hell.

Michael and I had been leading increasingly separate lives. My singing took me away a lot, and I increasingly moved in a younger set than he did. Michael still enjoyed pub culture, which I never joined in. We were good friends but we wanted different things. After long discussions, and with no animosity, we decided to go our own ways. I did not know where I was going to live after Michael sold the flat, but I was not worried. Life would show me the way. It always did.

Ironically, just as my personal life was coming apart, my legal status was confirmed. After eight long years, on 6 July 2005 (coincidentally the Dalai Lama's seventieth birthday), I was finally given British citizenship. It meant so much to me to be accepted at last. I dressed up in a midnight-blue velvet *cheong sam* dress that my mother-in-law had given me, and went with Michael to the town hall in Hove to receive my certificate.

I was very moved by the ceremony. In that room were old people, little children, the ugly and the infirm – and the British government was giving us all citizenship. This is truly spiritual, I thought, and I cried on behalf of us all. They gave us tea, coffee and snacks, and a pen in a box. I immediately laminated my certificate and hung it on the wall. I was no longer a ghost.

Technically, having Deckyi with me was now a possibility. I had continued to phone her regularly and detected a small but discernible thawing in her attitude towards me. Our holiday together had not been easy but we were nevertheless building a bridge of familiarity. I think my acquired 'detachment' had successfully reduced the tension between us. My frequent calls and genuine concern over her welfare also perhaps persuaded her that my feelings were real.

Casually, I asked the next time I phoned whether she would like to come to England, if it were possible, and after thinking about it she said yes. I so wanted to give her the chance of a better life. I told her I was willing to buy her a ticket to New York so that she could see her father too. I still believe it is right she should have that option. She didn't say anything to that. I hadn't spoken to Tenzin since the night he gave me Deckyi's phone number. He is married to another woman and our karma together is finished. If Deckyi wants to come, then my lovely mother-in-law, whom I see regularly, has said she can stay with her.

As of now I am leading a gypsy life once more. The flat is sold, I have packed my entire possessions into one suitcase, and I am living with a friend in London. I don't know where I will go next. I am not concerned. I have never planned ahead or thought of the future. I live for the day and wait to see where the winds of karma blow. I am a free spirit, and a nomadic lifestyle suits my nature. I have never had ambitions to own a house or possessions. My needs are few. I know I can earn money and will never starve.

That does not mean I don't have dreams. I haven't forgotten my wish to do some serious meditation – although if my daughter comes, that will have to be put on hold, as my first responsibility is to her. I yearn to see Tibet again – I miss the massive, rugged mountains, the vast open skies, the sense of limitless space, the sheer magnificent wildness of it all – and my people. Even if I don't make it in this lifetime, for years I have been collecting all my hair that has fallen, taking it from my comb, picking it up from the ground, with the idea that it be put on the sacred Shitak mountain where my mother was given her sky burial. I already have a big bag full. That way, a part of my body will be returned to Tibet.

Looking back at my life I can hardly believe all that has happened to me already. And right now I am standing on the edge of another mountain, waiting to jump.

Index